WHILE

I

HAVE

MY

BEING

2nd Edition

MICHELLE LOUISE PIERRE

ISBN-13: 978-1-7321274-0-1
ISBN-10: 1732127409

DEDICATION

First and foremost, this book is dedicated to my LORD and Savior, Jesus Christ, for without Him, I can do nothing. Secondly, it is being dedicated to four women, my spiritual daughters, Anna-Marie Calleros Valles, Leisl Griffith Redmond, Rosa Teran and Charmaigne Troutt-Jenkins, whose unconditional love, acceptance, and love for the LORD, inspires me to reach higher heights and deeper depths, as it further encourages me to strengthen my intimate relationship with the LORD along this Christian walk. I pray a blessing over them, and in Jesus' holy name, I ask that the LORD continuously surrounds them *(and their husbands, respectively, Sam, Charlie, Ben and Demetrius)* with His love and protection, as He orders their steps in ways that will bring Him ultimate glory that He, alone, is due! Amen!

Further, in loving memory of one of my very precious sisters in Christ, Angela "Angie" Torres, whose love knew no limits and whose smile not only lit up a room, but every heart it touched. I did it, girlllll!

To God be the glory!!!

March 15, 2018 – Thursday – Revised for 2ⁿᵈ Edition

ACKNOWLEDGMENTS

To acknowledge everyone who has ever been a source of encouragement to me would take an entire book to compile, so I will trust that you know who you are, and that you have my deepest gratitude. However, I will endeavor to list a few. To my confidants, for your unfailing support, because we love and accept one another, just the way that we are, warts and all. Also, to my personal champions, who could always be counted on to inspire me to push my creative envelope, one step further. To my former students *(and my master clinician/teacher, now friend, Rachel Mendoza, who taught me not only what I needed to know to be a successful Speech Therapist, but also what it truly looks like when a woman is totally in love with her husband),* aged three to twenty-one, who have provided, in their own special ways, inspiration that could only have come from God. To my family, and extended family, who each, in their own unique ways, have loved and supported me throughout the years. To my church family at New Hope Christian Fellowship Church *(truly a place of "Healing and Restoration")* for their love, acceptance and spiritual support. To my senior pastors, Victor Cervantes and Timothy Russell, men of deeply abiding faith and personal integrity, along with their wives, Cindee and Vanessa, respectively, whose love, encouragement and support, helped me to, again, step out on faith, embrace my calling and all of the gifts given to me by the LORD, for His glory! Further, to all of my countless e-mail and social media buddies, who have viewed my poems, short stories, commentaries, status messages and prayer requests, and have taken a moment to respond back.

Lastly, to two women, I lovingly refer to as "my number one fans", Sandy Solomon and Linda Lake, fellow sisters in Christ *(aka "biker babes", which then brings to mind my gal pal, Nora Lumia, and her husband, Jon).* Just thinking about your words of encouragement, kisses on the cheek and great, big, warm hugs, make me smile. May God continue to richly bless you and your husbands, Jim and Mike, respectively.

I sincerely appreciate and love you, all. Thank you!

March 5, 2018 – Monday – Revised for 2nd Edition

TABLE OF CONTENTS

INTRODUCTION

In 1995, I felt inspired to sit down and stop "giving away" to particular individuals, my poetry *(some of which, no doubt, has been lost to me, forever)*. The original book, <u>While I Have My Being</u>, contained seventy-seven poems. In this second edition, some have been re-edited and reformatted. In addition to that, it now contains three new poems written in 2017. The original title of this body of work, "Fire Burning In My Soul", was changed one Friday, in November of 1998, after reading Psalm 104, and having verse thirty-three seemingly jump right out at me! This majority of this book was written over the course of two years, beginning in October of 1998, when I wrote the first poem entitled, "Switch In The Spirit" to its conclusion, with the signature poem, "While I Have My Being", written on October 28, 2000. The three additional poems in this second edition, were written from September 8, 2017 to October 2, 2017. There is also a new section in the back entitled, "Notes and/or Insights", added in this edition just for you.

This work is a compilation of poetic verses, offered up as praise and worship to the LORD, Jesus Christ, as led and inspired by the Holy Spirit. At times, when thinking about what the LORD had brought me through, as the praise flowed through my soul, I would just begin to weep and/or sing aloud to myself. At other times, verses and lines of poetry would cascade through my mind, in such a persistent way, that I knew I must capture them in writing. In the process of writing this book, several other books were also being compiled. As God led, I would place a poem, as it took on shape and form, into whatever book I felt was most appropriate for it. This book, to me, is in concrete form, something that takes me back to those intimate places of praise and worship. At times, within this creative process, I would be working on up to three poems, simultaneously. Then, on a few occasions, I would find myself sitting in front of my computer, or with an actual paper writing tablet, when absolutely nothing would come, and no amount of trying to "work it up", would work. In so doing, I have learned to go with the LORD's flow, when He is moving, and to relax, thereby, investing time in other activities, when He is not. In the reading, I invite you to enter in with me. The poems are dated, so that you can journey along with me, with anchor points.

I view the writing of these poems as a ministry that God has so graciously blessed with me. It further blesses my heart when I have been approached by those, who have been touched, or challenged, in some way, by my muses. Over the years, I have either e-mailed, mailed or hand delivered poetry from these various books, to those in whom I could sense a personal need to hear a specific "right now" Word from the LORD. More often than not, it was simply the LORD knocking on the door of my heart, that brought about verses being formed into individual poems. If you have been privy to receiving some of my poetry, over the years, and do not see your favorite one(s) here, it is more than likely in one of my other completed works: <u>Altars of Praise, Worship, Healing and Deliverance</u> (1990 - 1996, majority written 1996), <u>Speaking In The Light</u> (1996 - 1998), <u>The God Of All Comfort</u> (1996 - 1998), <u>A Pen Of Iron</u> (1995 - 2000) and <u>The Heart Of A Poet</u> (1998 - 2000); or, in one of the other five books of poetry that are now being written, simultaneously: <u>A Consuming Fire</u>, <u>A Friend Loveth</u>, <u>As For Me And My House</u>, <u>Strength In My Soul</u> and <u>In A Solitary Way</u>, which is actually slated to be published next *(It is geared specifically towards Christian singles)*. Sooner or later, these books, and more, will also be published. Now that I have retired, I feel it is time to bring these books out of retirement, as well. ;-)

I pray the poems shared with you in <u>While I Have My Being – 2</u>nd <u>Edition</u>, will bless your heart and soul in the reading and ingesting, as much as they have blessed me in the writing. To God be the glory!!! Amen!!!

In His Devoted Love & Service,
Michelle Louise Pierre
*March 27, 2002 – Wednesday – 1*st *Edition*
*March 17, 2018 – Saturday – Revised for 2*nd *Edition*

PSALM 104: 27-33

These wait all upon thee; that thou mayest give them their meat in due season. That thou givest them they gather: thou openest thine hand, they are filled with good. Thou hidest thy face, they are troubled: thou takest away their breath, they die, and return to their dust. Thou sendest forth thy spirit, they are created: and thou renewest the face of the earth. The glory of the LORD shall endure for ever: the LORD shall rejoice in his works. He looketh on the earth, and it trembleth:

he toucheth the hills, and they smoke.

I will sing unto the LORD as long as I live: I will sing praise to my God while I have my being.

THE

POET

SINGS...

A PRAISE

I am so on the edge
Sunday service has not even begun
But, my heart is racing, animated in my chest
For to me, Jesus has already come
I am caught up completely in the praise

I can hear my Savior sweetly saying
Let not your hearts be troubled
Neither let them be dismayed
For, only, I will love you throughout eternity
My response, "You will always be worthy of the praise"

There is such a sweet Spirit in this place
It is calm, magnificent and receptive
God is ever so patiently pouring out His grace
Have Your way, sweet precious Lord
The Holy Trinity will be glorified in our praise

Hallelujahs ring so pleasantly in the air
We sing, hallelujahs to You, Almighty Lord
We have come to glorify Your name in this earth
Break up the fallow ground of our hearts
That way, we can more fully give You all of the praise

I worship and adore You, Father of mercy and of life
I pour out my heart before You as a morning sacrifice
Let it flow humbly before Your throne, oh Holy One
I bow my knee to You, overshadowed by the presence of Your Son
Make me, mold me, and continue to use me as an instrument of Your praise

October 19, 1998 - Monday

AN ATTITUDE OF GRATITUDE

Lord, I thank You
Lord, I thank You
Lord, I thank You

You have been so good to me
Your Holy Spirit, I desire to see
Your Son, alone, died to set me free

Father, God, what magnificent deliverance, Your hands have wroth
Your sweet savor flows through my soul, like a warm, healing broth
Your love, bubbling over in my heart, like root beer froth

Mighty, mighty King of glory
Thank You, Abba, for rewriting my story
You gave me joy, in place of a life of the ugly and gory

Blessings to You, the Savior of my soul
Blessings to You, Master, I give You full control
Blessings to You, Comforter, lovingly in Your arms, me enfold

I am Your masterpiece, formed by Your divine hands
Teach me to not be blown over by the storms as I, on You, stand
Glory, glory, hallelujah, thank You for being my Man

Thank You, for restoring the cracks and broken places that had made me so crude
Thank You, for teaching me that my praise and worship of You, determines my altitude
Thank You, for humbling my attitude, so that it will always be one of gratitude

May 30, 1999 - Sunday

BECAUSE HE LIVES

Life once defeated, now victorious
Heart once broken, now mended
Dreams once shattered, now restored
Hope once deferred, now here
Salvation once unknown, now pursued
Ears once flattered, now discerning
Soul once condemned, now comforted

Self once exalted, now sanctified
Ego once reigning, now demoted
Feelings once unwanted, now welcomed
Spirit once saddened, now joyous
Door once closed, now opened
Desires once fleshly, now submitted
Soul once empty, now filled

Lifestyle once erratic, now ordered
Spirit once quenched, now lit
Prayers once rote, now inspired
Love once deadened, now enlivened
Mind once unstable, now renewed
Shepherd once ignored, now followed
Soul once downcast, now revived

Body once dominating, now warring
Enemy once controlling, now rebuked
Faith once shaky, now impenetrable
Healing once unnecessary, now delivered
Feet once running, now planted
Eyes once roaming, now focused
Soul once emaciated, now satisfied

Child once playing, now matured
Christ once outside, now abiding
Tongue once uncontrollable, now tempered
Pride once raging, now humbled
Wisdom once blinded, now embraced
God once ignored, now glorified
Soul once lost, now found

Veil once permanent, now Christian
Realization once darkened, now enlightened
Bible once unread, now ingested
Jesus once ethereal, now Savior
Comforter once silenced, now directing
Father once tolerated, now LORD
Soul once tormented, now free

Why?
Because He lives, in me

June 20, 2000 - Tuesday

BEING TUCKED IN

Psalm 4: 8
I will both lay me down in peace, and sleep:
for thou, LORD, only makest me dwell in safety.

Proverbs 3: 21 - 26,
My son, let not them depart from thine eyes: keep sound wisdom and discretion: So shall
they be life unto thy soul, and grace to thy neck. Then shalt thou walk in thy way safely,
and thy foot shall not stumble. When thou liest down, thou shalt not be afraid:
yea, thou shalt lie down, and thy sleep shall be sweet. Be not afraid of
sudden fear, neither of the desolation of the wicked, when it cometh. For the
LORD shall be thy confidence, and shall keep thy foot from being taken.

Sweet blessed peace, the kind that only a true child of God, can experience
Abba reaching down, soothing out the rough edges of the day
Tenderly, lovingly touching your brow, caressing your soul, soothing your spirit

You, in response, repenting for things done wrong during your waking hours
Sometimes, seeking forgiveness for things left unsaid, deeds left undone
Receiving that loving forgiveness, along with that day's lessons in wisdom

There is nothing like His magnificent, unspeakably joyous, nestling hand of love
As if that is not enough, Jesus enters the room, bringing even more love with Him
Also, bringing light beyond measure, that humbles the soul even further in gratitude

Curling under those blankets, allowing yourself to be enveloped in a satisfying warmth
The Comforter has come, too, washing your soul with the confident love of obedience
Obedience learned while following Jesus' example, as you were led by the Holy Ghost

The stresses of the day are passing and the heavenly hosts stand guard over you
They have no power of their own, only what their Creator, our Father, allows them
Yet, knowing that He has sent them for your protection, closes your eyes in rest

Pleading the blood of Jesus, over your whole household, both, indoors and out
Slumber comes, as words of love and gratitude tumble naturally through your soul
Sweet sleep is your gift from God, the Father of mercy, love and all comfort

Now, thank Him, once more and close your eyes for the night
You can rest assured that, if He had ordained it to be so
New lessons will await the morning light

January 27, 2000 - Thursday

BLESS YOU

God, bless You
May my worship always be done in Spirit and in truth
May You always be blessed by my praise
May I willingly in love, this voice, in Your honor, raise

Because of Your unconditional love, Dear Father, Son and Holy Spirit
A song of gratitude from my heart is overflowing, I know You can hear it
Be blessed today, precious Holy One and forever draw me nearer
Compared to You, there is simply no one, I will ever hold dearer

I seem to seek Your blessings, more than I seek to bless Your heart
Bring me to the knees of my heart, as I submit, vowing never to depart
Turn me around continuously, Lord, for to You, I desire to remain faithful
Lord, may I always say, "Thank You", to You because I am so grateful

You did not have to do the things, You have so lovingly done for me
Not only was Your grace sufficient, but You restored my lost joy so beautifully
I could be insane, right now, or buried in my grave, with no hope of a new life
Yet, You asked admittance into my heart, freeing me from a tortuous time of strife

To simply say, "Thank You" and/or "Praise the Lord" never seems quite enough
Lord, You swooped right in and cleared out a lot of broken, self-destructive stuff
I owe You, not only for my life on this earth, but for the greatest gift of all
When the trump sounds for me, I will be able to rise upward to You holy call

Then, I will be able to give You my love, face to face
Then, I will be able to sufficiently thank You for Your grace
Then, I will have arrived at the home, this life was destined to bring me, too
Then, I will bow down at Your feet, in reverence and holiness to just bless You

June 15, 2000 - Thursday

BLOOD COVERING

Covered by the blood,
saturated in His sweet love.
Fire way down deep in my
soul, kindled by God above.

His Son's blood is
what I am talking about.
I do not want any confusion,
leave no room for doubt.

That blood was shed
on Golgotha's hill.
That blood has freed me
to do my Father's will.

The Holy Ghost has been given
to me to show me, my King.
He prompts my heart to pray, giving
my soul songs of deliverance to sing.

That blood has placed a hammer
in my hand, ready to pound stone.
No longer confused, sickness in
my body, has to leave me alone.

Prompted by the voice within,
anoint my own head with oil and pray.
Blessed victory, sickness gone,
this season, to await another day.

That blood strengthened when I
felt challenged beyond endurance.
Submitted to the Lord, pled the blood,
against which nothing can take a stance.

Thank You, Abba, for the Holy Spirit's
gentle, persistent residential hovering.
Thank You, Jesus, for Your death, burial and
Resurrection, left us this holy blood covering.

April 20, 2000 - Thursday

COVERED IN BLOOD,
SURRENDERED TO LOVE

Covered in blood
Surrendered to love
Help me, stay my course
Out of love, not force

Lord, strip me bare
I no longer care
Emotions, no longer sway
Teach me to, sincerely, pray

Jesus is my Lord
Strengthen this threefold cord
Holy Ghost, comfort and heal
In humble submission, I kneel

Abba's love enlivens, surrounds
No more time for inward frowns
Joy has found its target, my heart
Jump starting my day, I am set apart

Comforted by the only One, who can
Etched in the palm of His omnipotent hand
Protected by Jesus' blood
Surrendered to the Almighty's love

October 15, 1999 - Friday

DADDY'S ARMS

PSALM 142: 1 - 4 says, "I cried unto the LORD with my voice; with my voice unto the LORD did I make my supplication. I poured out my complaint before him; I showed before him my trouble. When my spirit was overwhelmed within me, then thou knewest my path. In the way wherein I walked have they privily laid a snare for me. I looked on my right hand, and beheld, but there was no man that would know me: refuge failed me; no man cared for my soul.".

I am hurting deep inside, and You have
brought me to this place for a reason.
I have also been forced to realize that no man can,
or will, be of comfort to me during this season.

You have ordained this to be so because
this is a time that You and I must spend, alone.
You have predestined it as a time, that cyclically comes,
of healing and deliverance, that will turn up all stones.

Whatever it is that You wish to show me,
I know that Your Son will be right there with me.
My flesh has grown weary of fighting losing battles,
so it's trying to convince me to throw in the towel and flee.

I will not leave this spot, until victory as declared
by You, Father, is at long last, completely mine.
This conflict has been raging for years,
the end is near, I will no longer be blind.

I know that the strength I need, can only come
coursing through my veins, with You, as its source.
You have told me that we have already won this victory;
we are storming the gates, taking my life back by force.

This time, is not a time for timidity or apathy's subtle enticements
to join hands with me, so that they can redirect me back to hell.
Gird up my loins, oh Lord, with righteousness and holiness,
the true companions, I will need to conquer this enemy and prevail.

Lord, You are totally awesome; I stand
ready and waiting, for Your divine revelation.
I have always felt this weight upon my shoulders, coming
and going, momentarily lifting, since my earthly creation.

Now, I realize that before this new season of my life can begin,
this needs to be completely dealt with and destroyed.
At its root, has been the self-pity of rejection, always there
to remind me, that I was once, willingly, the enemy's toy.

There is nothing like trying to do right, that will infuriate the enemy
to the point, where he will dig through all the old, locked cabinet doors.
As he digs, I look on, as if in a dream, standing helplessly by,
while he dumps, one by one, all of my garbage out onto the floors.

Snap out of complacency's death hold, for those things should
no longer torment me, fueling the flames of guilt and shame.
Plead the blood of Jesus against them, put the cross in his face;
he is already defeated and he has to acquiesce to King Jesus' name.

Victory, sweet victory, oh how sweet the glorious,
cleansing rain of grace and mercy are to my soul.
I have more than survived this attack, I am one
more precious step closer to being totally whole.

Thank You, Holy Ghost, blessed Comforter, for accompanying
me on every one of these, formerly soul-numbing, trips.
Thank You, Abba, for encouraging me to run into Your arms,
this day, speaking to no one but You, with these lips.

I am blessed to know You so intimately, Dear Father, and I cannot
adequately express the joyous, liberating affect that, that love has had on me.
All that I can say, is that I found out something very important today;
when I am hurting, there is no safer place to be, than in the arms of my Daddy.

June 6, 1999 – Sunday

ENGAGE MY HEART, OH LORD

Jeremiah 30: 19 & 20, 21b - 22, "And out of them shall proceed thanksgiving and the voice of them that make merry: and I will multiply them, and they shall not be few; I will also glorify them, and they shall not be small. Their children also shall be as aforetime, and their congregation shall be established before me, and I will punish all that oppress them. ... and I will cause him to draw near, and he shall approach unto me: for who is this that engaged his heart to approach unto me? saith the LORD. And ye shall be my people, and I will be your God."

Engage my heart, oh Lord, I pray.
Show me the way to faithfully stay.

Committed to the work, You have lain before me.
Snatching souls from hell's flame, with victory.

Power enabled, fueled by Your most holy hand.
Not concerned with nationality, or from what land.

Engage my heart, oh Lord, to do Your will.
Light a fire under me Lord, let me not always be still.

Still me, only when I need to listen more intently to You.
I cannot go forward, until You have told me what to do.

Give me the heart that I need, as I humbly prepare.
Show me, what I must do to, upon You, cast all my cares.

Engage my heart, oh Lord, to sing praise nonstop.
Lead me beyond the point where others may drop.

Fill me with Your compassion so that I will love as You lead.
Touching the souls, who are lost, discerning their true need.

Their need is for Jesus, the Savior, whom I have mercifully found.
The One, who took a shattered life and turned it around.

Engage my heart, oh Lord, to worship with abandonment.
Never let me forget, it was Your flesh that was rent.

Make me a living demonstration of the power of Your grace.
I sincerely desire with all of my heart, to see You, one day, face to face.

Bind Your Word to my heart with Your heavenly threefold cord.
Let these lips ever say, "Have Your way, engage my heart, oh Lord".

June 24, 2000 - Saturday

ESCAPING SOUL

Psalm 124: 7 & 8
Our soul is escaped as a bird out of the snare of the fowlers:
the snare is broken, and we are escaped. Our help is in the
name of the LORD, who made heaven and earth.

In comes a mighty,
rushing wind.
In that wind,
whispering of a Friend.

. . .

Blowing through my heart,
scattering all ungodly things.
Freeing me to listen, as a new song
my soul barely begins to sing.

Bringing a lightness and before
unknown joy, to my very countenance.
Knowing deep within, that I must
reach a place of true repentance.

Yet, still clinging to the things of this
world, as if caught in its death grip.
Not fully wanting to surrender, just
in case I might need to take a side trip.

. . .

Single and running to and fro, claiming
one thing one minute, and then another.
Lusting after a man, who should have
been seen as only a wounded brother.

Falling, falling, this time without what
was previously perceived as my safety net.
Knowing that I needed to get out of that
situation, in the accusing face of regret.

Doggedly pursued by shame and
accusation, as I ran for unsure cover.
Hiding out in the darkness of the lost,
longing for my soul's true Lover.

. . .

Coming to my senses, briefly caught in
the unrelenting, taunting voice of despair.
Hearing that wind come, again, telling me
that this Friend of my soul, did still care.

Repenting, in broken heartedness like a
foolish virgin, with no oil left in her lamp.
Surrendering to the Holy One, who has
come to take me out of the enemy's camp.

Assuring my heart that once forgiven, my
sins would be scattered to the four winds.
Clinging to the hand of my Master, who is
showing me how this life, anew to begin.

. . .

Thank You, Lord for wooing me, until I could
come to the place of heavenly new birth.
And, for helping my soul to escape the snares
of the fowler, before leaving this earth.

October 28, 2000 – Saturday

15

FATHER GOD, MAY ...

Father God, I give You all
of the honor, glory and praise.

May I worship You with
my life, all of my days.

May everything about me be
pleasing to You, including my ways.

May my heart long only to ultimately,
upon Your heavenly face, gaze.

May I always long for Your
tender touch, to be my mainstay.

May I forever remember that Your Son,
Jesus, on my behalf, constantly prays.

May I, now covered by Jesus' blood, be
challenged to go further through life's maze.

May I know with a blessed assurance that
for all of my sins, that blood still pays.

May my hands never be idle, as You
teach me, in submission, them to raise.

May words always be given to me by
You as we, together, coin each phrase.

May I allow the Holy Ghost to comfort my heart,
when going through a necessary down phase.

May I see clearly through Your eyes,
as You break down for me, this haze.

May I, as I sit on this rock face, continue to
speak to You of my tomorrow and yesterdays.

Father God, in heaven, I adore You.
Please, accept this word gift, as my humble praise.

Be Blessed, Oh Lord, Amen.

July 8, 2000 - Friday

FIGHT, ON YOUR KNEES!

The battle is violently raging
The wind of decision, blowing in
Confusion raining down
Controlling mind, thoughts
Tormenting soul, twisting psyche
Fear clutching, squeezing
Cementing its chilling hold

Restless sleep, no dreams
Nightmares on mind's screen
Caught in the grip of sin
Deceived by pride's longing heart
No one will know, should know
Cover up lie, for repentance, there is no need
Wrong veiled, in darkness' beguiling lace

Can't hide from God, He always sees
Ask Him for forgiveness, the weight of sin flees
Jesus must be Savior and Lord, no other frees
In His omnipotent hands, alone, resides the keys
Learning you can no longer do, whatever you please
Stop giving into your flesh, in all of its subtle degrees
This battle, must continue to be fought, on your knees

June 6, 1999 - Sunday

FILL ME WITH YOUR FIRE, LORD

Fill me with Your fire, Lord, never let me burn cold.
Touch me with the wind of Your Spirit, Lord,
and never my hand, cease to hold.

My love for You knows no boundaries, no limits.
Help me to never do anything halfheartedly, for You,
for I must put my whole heart and soul in it.

Fill me, Lord, I feel a praise bubbling in my soul.
Remove those things from me that would, and have,
caused my love to run hot one minute, then cold.

The rhythm in my soul has now set my heart aflame.
Lord, have mercy, this joy is as no other;
it cannot be contained, for I must sing Your name.

Fill me Lord, so the wind of Your Spirit can wash me clean.
Use me for Your glory, humble my spirit through prayer and fasting,
so that I will continue to, on You, exclusively and wholeheartedly, lean.

My bones and my joints rise to the occasion, not wanting to be left out.
Show me how to kill this flesh, so that it gets no praise for itself, as I
use this body as an instrument of worship, leaving no room for doubt.

Thank You, for filling me, anew and even more gloriously, with Your fire, Lord.
Shackles have fallen to the ground, loosening the chains of bondage,
giving me a deeply rooted praise, that I can no longer, for myself, hoard.

May 29, 1999 - Saturday

FIRED UP!

Lord, this praise is bubbling,
churning in my soul.
My heart is listening to the
greatest story ever told.

True it is, not an
ounce of fiction here.
Open up the ears of
your heart, draw near.

God came in the flesh,
Jesus is His name.
Only Begotten Son of the Father,
healing the crippled, the lame.

He walked this earth as
a man for many years.
Blessed be the name of the
Lord, praise Him, can't you hear?

Hear the mighty rushing wind of praise,
flooding the depths of my being.
When you see that light beaming out
from my eyes, don't think of fleeing.

That light is not mine, so don't be
jealous of me, to it, I can lay no claim.
It was given to me as a free gift, when
I began to call on the Savior's name.

The same light that you see in me,
and others, who are His children, too.
Is just as freely available, with the stipulation
that Jesus becomes Savior, to you.

He is giving out blessings and the oil of the
Holy Ghost is overflowing from my cup.
Hallelujah! Praise His holy name! My
heart is bursting with joy, I am fired up!

April 1, 1999 - Thursday

FRESH, NEW START

Loving touch, once,
home of my heart.
Turn me back Lord,
I need a fresh start.

I have stumbled, despair
has gotten a vital hold.
My love for Your people,
has gone strangely cold.

That situation knocked me
down, taking me for a loop.
I almost completely reverted to type,
and locked the door of my coop.

But, the love that You had already
placed in my soul, would not be still.
I could no longer be comfortable in the
darkness; for, I have tasted of Your will.

That love bubbled through my heart,
and began to show, again, from my eyes.
Now, I can participate in this life, anew,
because more of my flesh has had to die.

Thank You, for rejuvenating and restoring
that love, now percolating in my heart.
Blessed be Your name, Jesus; my soul is
bursting with joy, due to my fresh, new start.

May 26, 1999 - Wednesday

FULL OF HIS GOODNESS

Psalm 33: 5b
...the earth is full of the goodness of the LORD.

The trees sway to the beat of heaven
The birds sing sweetly to the tune that the angels make
The grass stands tall and straight, applauding His Majesty
The dirt lies flatly, prostrate under the Master's care
The flowers come, in their time, springing forth in worship and praise

The tides, ebb and flow, cyclically, bringing life and death to the land
The ocean waves crash against the shore, molding it to God's design
The rivers run, sweeping away the drift wood, like the Lord's hand on your life
The clouds shape and reshape, giving us images that soothe, comfort and convict
The lightning and thunder roll, showing how Jesus pierces darkness, with light

The insects till the soil, preparing it for new life to sprout forth, in its season
The chameleon changes colors, for protection, witnessing to the facets of Abba's care
The lion, roaring at night, disturbing the calm, like a wake-up call from the Holy Spirit
The baby birds, with mouths open wide, demonstrating our posture before the Father
The kitten's gentle purring, at touch, speaking volumes about a contented soul

Yes, the earth is truly full of the goodness of the Lord
Blessed be the name of the Lord, God Almighty

April 16, 1999 - Wednesday

21

FURNACE BUILDING FAITH

Isaiah 48: 8 - 10
Yea, thou heardest not; yea, thou knewest not; yea, from that time that thine ear
was not opened: for I knew that thou wouldest deal very treacherously, and wast
called a transgressor from the womb. For my name's sake will I defer mine anger,
and for my praise will I refrain for thee, that I cut thee not off. Behold, I have
refined thee, but not with silver; I have chosen thee in the furnace of affliction.

Wow, Lord, it is hot in here
I do not like it in this place
Sweat popping out on my brow
Knots forming in my stomach
Chills running down my spine
Depression seeping in, between the cracks
Self-pity weighing me down
Cannot take the pressure anymore
Want to run and hide, trapped
Who would really notice?
Just slip quietly out of the back door
Sink into the suffocating arms of despair

Faith challenged, down to my toes
Thought I knew all the answers
Intellectualizing, all my moves
Thinking quicker than the average Joe
Flesh on parade, at all times
Smile plastered on the face, just so
Mask on straight, not crooked
Knowing all of the right turns, signals
All of the right words to say
Timing down to an act of science
Perfection gleaming from my face
Darkness hidden, by a false light

Happily going on
Oblivious to my eternal fate
Fate, what's that, I'll make my own, anyway
Friends galore, only those, who will sing my praise
Outward beauty, veiling the ugliness within
People vying for my attention
Everyone wants to be my friend
Head so puffed up, I float into a room
Vanity, my constant, ego building, companion
Dressed in just the right clothes
Not one hair out of place
Not ever reading the Bible words, I profess

Who really has time for God?
He expects, demands much, too much
Tired of being nice to people, I don't really like
I am sleepy, I won't go to church today
God understands my weaknesses, my frailties
Louis got on my nerves, I told him off, but good
Now, he knows to stay away from me
I asked God for forgiveness, that's enough
He was a little weasel, anyway
That association needed to end
Now, he's walking around trying to look wounded
He needs to get over it, get a life

.   .   .

Oh my God, I just lost my job
My mate has said, "Good-bye"
I am desperately alone
Even my faithful friends no longer come
My props have been destroyed, annihilated, gone
My health is deteriorating
To whom can I turn? No one returns my calls
Shame and reproach, cover my head
Bible doesn't look so stupid now
I reach for it, in the night stand drawer
I read, I weep, I repent, I call on God
The still small voice of the Lord, answers

.   .   .

Humility sweeps over me, causing me to bend
A light comes on, in my soul, removing darkness' den
Showing me the type of hell I have been in
Revealing the kind of people, I had called, friend
Lord, I was on my way to hell, led there by my sin
Your touch, opening the eyes of my soul to deception's grin

That grin strangely familiar, had it once been on my face?
Crushed and broken beyond measure, now letting You be in first place
Thank You, Holy Father, for blessing me with the hand of Your grace
Thank You, sweet Jesus, for burning off the dross that had occupied my space
Thank You, Holy Ghost, for rescuing me, before I could hell, fully taste
Most of all, Dear Lord, thank You for putting me in this furnace, to build my faith

May 29, 1999 – Saturday

GENTLENESS

2 Samuel 22: 36
Thou hast also given me the shield of thy salvation:
and thy gentleness hath made me great.

Subtle tones of persuasion
Seeking entrance to my soul
A gentle knock on the door
Trying desperately to seek a foothold

Who is that gentle Spirit
Blowing so sweetly and lovingly in my direction
Breathing life into my weary mind, tired body
Soothing my heart with His gentle corrective affection

Never forcing or manipulating
Causing my heart to stir, to yearn
Standing patiently by
Only wanting, my love in return

He has become my love, soul, heart, life
He fills the crevices of my spirit, untouched by man
This love is so precious, so divine
Thank You, Father, for making me a part of Your plan

I love You, beyond the seas, the skies
It is in Your arms of eternity, where I belong
Knowing with all certainty, in my contented heart
It is Your gentleness that has truly made me strong

November 24, 1998 – Tuesday

GOD SAID, "NO!"

Lamentations 3: 19 - 22,
Remembering mine affliction and my misery, the wormwood and
the gall. My soul hath them still in remembrance, and is humbled in me.
This I recall to my mind, therefore have I hope. It is of the LORD'S
mercies that we are not consumed, because his compassions fail not.
They are new every morning: great is thy faithfulness.

Dying inside
Emotional suicide
Nowhere left to hide
Go on, take that, over the cliff, ride
Leave a note, next to the bedside
Wake up call from the throne of grace
God said, "No!"

Little baby sleeping, six months old
Fever raging inside, body burning hot then cold
Left alone in the room, no one to hold
Blankets soaked, darkness begins to enfold
Marked by the enemy to die, story untold
Wake up call from the throne of predestination
God said, "No!"

Three years old now, crippled emotionally, before all
Playmates, simply shadows on the wall
In the darkness, comfortable, alone in the hall
Wanting to be alone, choosing on no one, to call
Learned to comfort oneself, when hurt after a fall
Wake up call from the throne of light
God said, "No!"

Seven years old, late one night, lying awake in bed
Night terrors stalking, sinister, coated with black and red
Heart beating wildly in that small chest, pounding in the head
Confused by the horror, siblings sleeping, look dead
Going insane, a drop at a time, light penetrates the room instead
Wake up call from the throne of peace
God said, "No!"

25

Ten years old, taken on a long trip
Abandonment felt, tears flow, quivering on the lip
Parental love gone, life has taken a devastating dip
Not a lap child, not one to hang on someone's hip
Troubling thoughts, paranoia, almost causing the mind to flip
Wake up call from the throne of compassion
God said, "No!"

Twelve years old, lying disheveled on that cold kitchen floor
Attacked from the back, by a relative, while doing a chore
Praying for your life, yet, not wanting to take it anymore
Choked within inches of death, head banged on the linoleum, once more
Seeing a light at the end of the tunnel, running through the front door
Wake up call from the throne of love and clarity
God said, "No!"

Seventeen years old, cute as a button, with very little foresight
Trying to get home from work, in the dead of the night
At a bus stop, waiting for the next connection, standing under a light
Strange men, milling all around, trying to look brave with all your might
A brotherly figure approaches, protecting you, until the bus comes within sight
Wake up call from the throne of wisdom and understanding
God said, "No!"

Twenty-third birthday, driving away from party, heading for home
Light changes green, broad-sided by another car, hearing the impact of chrome
Life flashes before your eyes, mind blinded by headlights, begins to roam
Glass and other debris filters through your hair, like a comb
Securely protected, in the car bent in half, like fragile eggs in a carton of Styrofoam
Wake up call from the throne of might and power
God said, "No!"

• • •

All of these situations were set up to take my mind, my life and eventually my soul
I will sing, write and speak my testimony of deliverance, as I continue, in Him, to grow
Hallelujah! Praise the name of the Lord! Jesus is real! In each case, God said, "No!"

Even in the smallest way, in everything I do, think and say, oh Dear Lord
May it all be a testimony to Your loving mercy and grace in my life, this day
Blessed be Your holy name, keep me under the shadow of Your wings, I pray

For surely, it is by Your lovingly tender mercies that I was not consumed
Many spoke death over my life and, even, tried to end it, long ago
But, praise God, hallelujah, because You, Dear Father, said, "No!"

May 18, 1999 – Tuesday

HALLELUJAH, BLESS YOU, OH LORD

For all the times, You've
been there for me
For all the rescues, You've
allowed me to see.

For times so sweet and pure
they could be only shared alone
For the moments of sweet caress
You've given me, right down to the bone

For saving my soul, giving me back my song
creating me anew, and healing me, too
For deliverance wroth, seen and unseen, that
the Holy Ghost tenderly brought me through

For Your sweet Son, Jesus, my provider
divine keeper and lover of my soul
For You, Abba, my Creator, who made me
not fragmented and broken, but whole

For all Your commands that kept me, even
shakily, at times, walking on this righteous path
For the blessed washing of body and soul
to the core of my being, saving me from wrath

But, most of all, thank You for the Holy Ghost
who teaches me how on this rock, to stay
Bless You, for Your secure, unconditional love
that is, now, firmly planted in my heart, today

HALLELUJAH
BLESS YOU
MY LORD
MY GOD
JEHOVAH...

June 1, 1999- Tuesday

HE HAS RISEN!

Matthew 28: 6 & 7
He is not here: for he is risen, as he said. Come, see the
place where the Lord lay. And go quickly, and tell his
disciples that he is risen from the dead; and, behold, he goeth
before you into Galilee; there shall ye see him: lo, I have told you.

Hey, have you not heard, He has risen!
His death purchased our way out of hell's prison.

These plans were set in stone before the world began.
They agreed, He would come into this world as a man.

He was to walk this earth and blend right in.
Not in all ways, though, He was to live a life, free of sin.

Cheer up, step lively, let all the saints proclaim.
His resurrected life, has secured for us a new name.

We can now proudly say, "I am a Christian", without any doubt.
Come now, fellow soldiers in this army, let's give out a shout!

He is our Savior, Deliverer and Lord, throughout infinity.
He is also an integral part of the Holy Trinity.

Hey, celebration time is here, again, this blessed Easter season.
Because He rose that third day, my life now has purpose, love and reason.

His resurrected life, guaranteed our victory over death, hell and the grave.
This joyous time, is set aside to acknowledge that blessed life, He so freely gave.

He gave it, so that He could rise again, with all power, sealed forever, in His hands.
Eat candy, dye eggs, if you must; forget not, that you are also a vital part of Their plans.

His name is Jesus, God's Son, Restorer of life, love, hope and vision.
Hey, have you not heard, He has risen!

March 31, 1999 - Wednesday

HE TURNED THE OTHER CHEEK

He, my darling Savior, turned
the other cheek, so why not I?
He didn't have to go to that cross to,
my sweet Jesus, in my place, die.

My problems seem monumental,
so I aggressively wrestle, toss and turn.
Now, in the light of His great sacrifice,
they merely become lessons to be learned.

Father, forgive me, this selfsame hour,
for I certainly do not always know what I do.
My hands and feet, not nail scarred, no bruises on my back,
appear minuscule, in the light of what You went through.

My skin has not been torn, nor my clothes
ripped from my body, leaving me exposed.
I marvel at the example that You placed before me,
in how to, in adversity and trial, keep my mouth closed.

Lord, grant me, this day, the Spirit of calm, peace and
a much more stable, sound temperament and mind.
Move me out of my own way as I surrender my life back
into Your hands; and, root out whatever impurities You find.

Find them, You will, for I am still very much in this earthly vessel, designed
to house the Spirit of the Most High God, who is indeed living and not dead.
Lord, help me, even in this need of repentance, to humble myself
before Your throne of mercy and grace, as more of this flesh, is shed.

Thank You, Lord, for these revelations that have caused my heart to stir
and tears to flow from eyes, that were once hardened, unable to be meek.
Thank You, for releasing me from the torment of always feeling on the defensive, by
consoling me with the loving fact that, the King of kings, chose to turn the other cheek.

April 3, 2000 - Monday

HELLO, SELF!

Love reunited, after so much time apart
Blessed in heart, body and soul
Learning to, tenderly, reach out in love to You
To fall in love with You and Your special touch
Lord, You have finally become my all and all

Sweet words of praise and adoration fill my mind
Love songs laid dormant for so many years
Words placed in my soul by You
Placed there before I was even a thought
Before, in fact, time could even begin

Tears spilling down my cheeks
Heart blessed to the max
Body warmed from the fire within
The fire of Your holy presence
Speaking lovingly to my mended heart

Created to praise You
Now, truly capable of fulfilling that role
Worshipping with wisdom, understanding
Not just for things done
For the You, whom You are to me

Restored back to the wholeness of my origin
The whole person, whom I was predestined to be
To be called holy, perfected at Your hand
Jesus' sacrificial loving blood, cleansing me along the way
Hallelujahs, flood my soul, causing my feet to dance

In loving gratitude to the Father, causing me to be twice born
Forgiving me, giving me another chance at happiness, joy
Learning to do things, this time, led on by the Holy Ghost
Healing me deeply, within the innermost chambers of my soul
Restoring not only the joy, reacquainting me with myself

The self, who You created me to be
The self, who longed so many years to be free
The self, who desired, even in darkness, to know Thee
The self, who almost gave up on life, but You did not give up on me
The self, who had no idea how sweet a godly life, with You, would truly be

March 15, 1999 - Monday

HIDE ME IN YOUR PAVILION, LORD

Psalm 27: 1, 3b - 5
The LORD is my light and my salvation; whom shall I fear? the
LORD is the strength of my life; of whom shall I be afraid? ... in this will I be confident.
One thing have I desired of the LORD, that will I seek after; that I may dwell in
the house of the LORD all the days of my life, to behold the beauty of the LORD,
and to inquire in his temple. For in the time of trouble he shall hide me in his pavilion:
in the secret of his tabernacle shall he hide me; he shall set me up upon a rock."

Hide me in Your pavilion, Lord, that I may
learn the psalms of worship and of praise.
Hide me in Your pavilion, Lord, that these tired,
worn out limbs may from earth's death grip, raise.

Teach me to war in the Spirit, while tapping into Your heart,
concerning the things that You have predestined for my life.
Teach me to humbly submit to Your authority, while learning
the wisdom of the ages gleaned from Your cup of sacrifice.

Place me upon the rock, in the safety of Your sanctuary where
I will learn from You, to preach and teach Your Word with authority.
While on that rock, Lord, further teach me, in humility, to do what
You preordained would be necessary for me, to fulfill my destiny.

Bring me to the place of understanding, and true acceptance, in knowing that I have
not been put on this earth to be ordinary, or moved by every wind and doctrine.
Lord, I know intellectually that this call is very different from the norm; help me to
accept it with my heart and willingly press on, not swayed by friend or kin.

Help me to do what You ask, in such a way that Your thoughts truly become mine,
and I stop feeling compelled to try to blend into every situation like a chameleon.
Lord, for only then will I automatically seek You, first, as I come to know You in
Your fullness and allow You, in times of need, to safely hide me in Your holy pavilion.

September 8, 2000 - Friday

HIS VOICE, MY MELODY

Isaiah 51: 3
For the LORD shall comfort Zion:
he will comfort all her waste places;
and he will make her wilderness like Eden,
and her desert like the garden of the LORD;
joy and gladness shall be found therein,
thanksgiving, and the voice of melody.

His life
My heart

His heart
My breath

His breath
My will

His will
My ways

His ways
My life

His life
My example

His example
My hope

His hope
My salvation

His salvation
My decision

His decision
My deliverance

His deliverance
My healing

His healing
My restoration

His restoration
My focus

His focus
My wholeness

His wholeness
My gift

His gift
My joy

His joy
My song

His song
My desire

His desire
My love

His love
My comfort

His comfort
My gladness

His gladness
My thanksgiving

His thanksgiving
My voice

His voice
My melody

June 16, 1999 - Wednesday

HOLD FAST!

Hebrews 10: 23
Let us hold fast the profession of our faith
without wavering; for he is faithful that promised.

Blessed be the name of the Lord,
for He is truly worthy to be praised!
Glorify His name from the mountain tops
to the valleys low, this sweet Saturday.

Lord, thank You, because Your divine, unswerving faithfulness
is bubbling up inside, changing this once routine, journal entry.
I can feel You moving through my spirit as Your warmth spreads
from head to toe, with the magnificence of Your love for me.

Dear Father of graciousness and mercy, I desire
to faithfully love You, with all that is within.
Keep the deliverances coming, sweet Jesus, forever
cleansing me, from the deadly stains of my sin.

Step in, right now, and set my feet on a sure, plain path,
because of my fleshly desires and the insipid voice of my adversaries.
Precious Holy Ghost, comfort and strengthen my heart as You turn me back around,
teaching me to shout victory's sweet battle song, right in the face of my enemies.

You have told me, that the battle that is raging all around me, is for the
ultimate possession of my soul, and it is being waged to seal my fate.
Lord, continue to build within me an unshakable determination
to stay on this preordained path of righteousness and not hesitate.

This time, moving forward, without all of the stumbles, for I know that I can
no longer afford to turn back, to sample the mistakes of my blood covered past.
Teach me how to hold onto the profession of my faith, without vacillating and wavering;
Sweet merciful Lord, teach me to trust You, beyond intellect, teach me how to hold fast.

October 16, 1999 - Saturday

34

HOLD ONTO YOUR HEALING

Dear Heart, hold onto your healing.
Certainly God, our Father, knows all of the hurts of your past,
that are still affecting your life, trying to maintain control of your feelings.

Hold on, my friend, and let the Lord, continue Hs perfecting work.
Don't give in and go back to that time in your life,
when you were running aimlessly around, going berserk.

Jesus came, died and rose to bring salvation's healing light to your battered soul.
This was sealed in heaven, by the presence of the Holy Ghost on this earth,
so grab on tightly, surrender to Him, do not let go of your hold.

Toss and turn, on your bed of lonely, affliction, if you must.
Just don't give into the enemy's ploys or decoys, certainly, you've
learned by now, that in his deceptive enticements, to no longer trust.

Rebuke him, in the name of Jesus, plead the blood over his deadly, corrupt heart.
Once gone, for this season, saturate your soulish mind in His Word, until from
your thoughts, this Word of love and devotion can no longer, again, depart.

With all that we have discussed and prayed about, I know that your mind is still reeling.
Know this, right now, I am praying, Dear One, that you will stay strong in the Lord,
and, continue to victoriously hold onto your God ordained healing.

March 23, 1999 - Tuesday

HOW DID YOU KNOW?

How did you know?
How did you know?
Rest in His love, child,
the Holy Ghost told me so.

Feeling unloved and under
appreciated, you need love today.
Lock the door of your office or go into the
bathroom, hug yourself, begin to pray.

You've allowed yourself to be taken advantage
of, again, and now your feel like a fool.
Don't go off on a temper tantrum, you are
a child of God, learn to keep your cool.

They looked at you funny and stopped
talking, when you entered the room.
Christ is still on the throne of your heart,
hold your head up, speak life, not doom.

Here comes "back stabber" with selective
memory, today, wanting to be your friend.
Lord, have mercy, because you remember
the day when that was you, lost in your sin.

A personal call, has made you want to
run for cover, or lash out at someone.
Hang in there, the Holy Spirit is coming to
the rescue, this battle, too, is already won.

Your boss just yelled at you, blaming you for
something you did not do, you want to quit.
Hold on, you have been placed there by the
Lord, only He can tell you when "to get".

Of all things, the one with the loud voice is
coming down the hall, interrupting your work.
This moment, too, will pass quickly, it is only a
light affliction, don't get irritated or go berserk.

Eyes all red, because you tossed and turned
all night, worried about today's outcome.
Not the smartest thing to do, but thank God,
He still helps us, even when we act dumb.

Abba wanted to rock you to sleep, but you
chose to hold onto your worries and doubts.
It's still not too late to lay them at His feet,
relinquish your hold, gracefully bow out.

Feeling loved and blessed, then your
coworker came over and started some mess.
Two seconds before a negative response,
conviction hit, causing you to de-stress.

Trying to work on your computer as "nosy"
comes in, nonchalantly, staring at the screen.
Take a few deep breaths, keep working,
this is the time to, on the Lord, more fully lean.

If one more person knocks, or calls you on
the phone, the Fourth of July will seem tame.
Say a prayer for a calming stillness in your
soul and spirit, do it now, in Jesus' name!

You have a lot of things to do after work, your
life has ceased to be fun, whom can you call?
Take a moment to thank our Father, Son, and
Holy Ghost, for this day's blessings, trials and all.

June 2, 1999 - Wednesday

I AM SO GRATEFUL

I am so grateful that I have
been allowed to see the dawning
of this new, wonderful, glorious day.
Thank You, Lord, for leaving me
on this earth, direct my heart in the
direction You desire me to pray.

Lightness encapsulates my heart,
as my mind twirls like a dancer,
whirling uninhibited to and fro.
I am free in my soul and refuse
to let bondage, again, come in
permanently, so it must go!

In the name of Jesus, I cast down
thoughts that have come to try and
give self-pity a place in my domain.
So, I did not get what I wanted that time,
obviously the Lord has something
better, that will permanently remain.

But for a fleeting moment, I allowed
those thoughts to stare back at me
from the mirror of accusation.
Blessed be the Lord, for the Holy Ghost
rose to the forefront, to remind me that
I am a member of Their most holy nation.

I am a precious child of the King of kings
and Lord of lords, who directs my steps
as carefully as a train moves along its track.
Abba has filled my cup so many times,
that ingratitude and self-pity have to flee
in the face of this frontal, godly attack.

Lord Jesus, thank You for always
being there for me and for rescuing me
in times of need, whether I knew it or not.
Thank You, Father, for giving me this well spring
of life that bubbles up in my soul, and by Your
grace, will never run cold or lukewarm, but hot.

Thank You, Dear Lord, for giving me free access to
Your throne of grace and mercy, where I can come boldly
and know I am freely welcomed, never having to intrude.
Thank You, for this life that You have so lovingly
blessed me with, and for nurturing in my heart a deeply
abiding love for You, wrapped up securely in my gratitude.

September 8, 2000 - Friday

I CAN FIX IT

Sweet baby, I still love you,
but go ahead and take a seat.
Let Me have control, for you have
forgotten the enemy's defeat.

Let me remind you, it is I, who
gave him permission to exist.
In point of fact, he can do nothing
that is not already on My list.

Child, do not be deceived, there
is truly, nothing new under the sun.
Jesus, came down to prove, once and
for all, this battle, I have already won.

Stay in that chair, rest your nerves,
your battle is not with flesh and bone.
How many times do I have to
tell you, to leave this one, alone?

Rest in Me, My child, and don't get up;
be at peace, right where you sit.
This one, get your hands off, leave
it completely to Me, for only I can fix it.

June 1, 1999 - Tuesday

I GOT BACK, MY SONG!

Sitting in a valley of dry, dry bones.
Fighting feelings of being all so alone.
Wondering what in the world could have gone so wrong.
Trying to give praise in the midst of a congregation, without my song.

Looking around at the others, seemingly lost in their praise.
The music's beat going higher, higher, still my hands do not raise.
Lord, what is going on around me and why can't I just join in?
Wanting to praise You with understanding, not just going off the deep end.

Something is out of order here, I can feel it in my spirit.
The pastor is beckoning to me from the altar, I do not want to go near it.
Someone has come to tug me by the arm, bringing me up to there, anyway.
Lord, I do not want to cause a scene, so I plead the blood as I begin to pray.

The pastor having summoned, has now decided not to lay hands on me.
I, in turn, stand there, silently praying, knowing under Your protection, I will be.
Time passes and I continue to talk to You as my mind tries to filter through the haze.
I look around, feeling like I am standing in the midst of some manic craze.

A few weeks later on my way back there, You speak to me of changing direction.
I ponder this over in my mind, instinctively knowing You are offering me correction.
I take the appropriate exit that will lead me to a place, where I have already been.
Hadn't been there for months, but when the praise arose, I was able to enter right in.

I sang along with the music, in a voice that I had thought was gone away, for good.
Realizing then, weights were dropping off of me, like a tumbling cord of wood.
A shout percolated inside my soul and spilled out of my mouth, like foam in a glass.
It came from a dormant place, I thought was buried, its day having come to past.

Well, hallelujah, praise the Lord, for I could feel it in my bones, I was back on track!
No longer was I trying to draw water from a well, that was not operating in the black.
I gulped in that divine blessing, finding it was the thing for which my soul did long.
With praise and joy overflowing, I could hear my spirit say, "I got back, my song!".

October 4, 2000 - Wednesday

I HOPE YOU DON'T MIND

I hope you don't mind, that I
Laugh too loud
Pray too long
Sing deliverance's song

I hope you don't mind, that I
Dance when moved
Raise hands high
Shout, holler, sigh

I hope you don't mind, that I
Ignore outside interference
Know Jesus' friendship
Acknowledge His Lordship

I hope you don't mind, that I
Abandon myself, freely
Have no shame
Call His name

I hope you don't mind, that I
Invite His Presence
Remain in anticipation
Minister without hesitation

I hope you don't mind, that I
Won't be hindered
Follow Abba's lead
Know my need

I hope you don't mind, that I
Stand on promises
Need His touch
Love Him, much

I hope you don't mind, that I
Pray for you
Cry sometimes, too
Will pray through
I hope you don't mind

November 25, 1999 - Thursday

I LOVE YOU, BECAUSE...

I love You, because You first loved me, demonstrating that love in so many ways.
That unadulterated love pulsates through my very being, healing, infusing my life with
wondrous pleasures and insights that bring clarity, where once there was only haze.

I love You, because of the love that You have birthed in my heart, for myself.
This love was by no means of the instantaneous variety, because before I could
even consciously feel it, it was locked away in a combination safe, on a back shelf.

I love You, because of the lightness that I feel in this soul, that causes my heart to soar.
This lightness still catches me by surprise, for so long, my life and the heaviness
that I felt in my spirit, was akin to a ship drifting aimlessly, just beyond shore.

I love You, because You built within me, brick by brick, a hope that now burns bright.
This hope has grown to such tremendous proportions, that You have actually
graced me, once lost in darkness myself, to now draw others to Your magnificent light.

I love You, because You, alone, sung lullabies to me in the dark, cold, lonely nights.
These lullabies soothed and comforted, peacefully washing over my soul, gently
teaching me that I was better than what they thought, and I was beautiful in Your sight.

I love You, because of the strong arms of support, You have always given freely to me.
Those strong arms held me up, when I felt that the blows that I had been dealt,
had surely crushed and destroyed all of the visions that You had allowed me to see.

I love You, because there used to be locations in my spirit that I would not even visit.
These locations, were hidden from me, by You, because You knew, in Your mercy,
that there was no way that I would survive that necessary trip, without the Holy Spirit.

I love You, most of all, because the blood of Jesus was shed to save my soul from hell.
That blood flowed, giving me a purpose and joy unspeakable as Your love, heavenly Father,
has given me the courage to reach out to others, not in a whisper, but a yell!

I love You, Dear Lord, because...

October 31, 1998 - Saturday

43

I PRESS

Philippians 3: 14
I press toward the mark for the prize of
the high calling of God in Christ Jesus.

Single
I press

Lonely
I press

Discouraged
I press

Biological-clock
I press

Childless
I press

Brokenhearted
I press

Confused
I press

•   •   •

I am Christ's
I press

I am anointed
I press

I am humbled
I press

I am saved
I press

I am sanctified
I press

I am Spirit-filled
I press

I am determined
I press

September 12, 1999 - Sunday

I REPENT

Hard as any nail
Soul imprisoned in jail

Set it free, not in compliance
Cannot do it alone, in the dark silence

Still small voice, familiar, not completely unknown
Been with me since childhood, now I am grown

Tired and weary, right done to the core
Nothing interests me any longer, it's all a bore

Help me Lord, I sincerely pray
I do not want to continue living this insipid way

Light from heaven, shining in the darkness, right before my eyes
Soul surrendered to the Savior's call, no longer destined to die

Eternal life promised, confession and acceptance of Jesus, the key
He stepped in right on time, changing my once self-destructive destiny

Now, soft as a kitten, purring sweetly, content
Vulnerable to all, and nothing, My Lord, forgive me, I repent.

June 1, 1999 - Tuesday

I WILL COMPLAIN,
NO MORE

I will complain,
no more

God had evened
the score

Jesus stepped in through
my open door

His flesh on the cross
they ripped, they tore

Now, I know what I
should be praising Him for

He brought salvation to my heart,
felt right down to the core

Serving Him, no longer done
like an obligation or a chore

I can praise Him, now, with
understanding and desire, for sure

You see, I love and trust Him, that's why,
I will complain, no more

May 26, 1999 - Wednesday

I WOKE UP THIS MORNING

I woke up this morning,
routinely, curling up into a ball.
Hugging myself and thanking
the Lord, for being my all and all.

Aston-Marie coming over for her morning
stroke of fur and purr session all around.
That done, I swing my feet over the side of
the bed, as on the floor, I place them down.

Standing to stretch upwards to heaven,
speaking lovingly to Jesus, the Lord of my heart.
Lifting up names to Him, as He places them on
my mind, before this day, I can really start.

Taking some time to allow Him the opportunity
to speak to me of the Word for the day.
Securing it in my heart, while doing morning
chores, that needed doing right away.

Settling in with the Bible on my lap,
reading the Word, calming my soul within.
Stopping from time to time, to allow Father's
words of wisdom and direction, to sink in.

Giving praise to the Lord, the lover of
my soul, as tears mist in my eyes.
Knowing full well without His grace and
mercy, I could have in the night, just died.

Obviously, He still has work for me to
do here, so on this earth I must stay.
Introspectively, I examine myself
for unconfessed sin in my life, I pray.

Focusing the intentions of my heart on the task
at hand, so the purging can fully take place.
For the desire of my heart is to one day see
my loving Savior, Jesus Christ, face to face.

Now, it's time to continue preparing for
work, as the sun shines on the horizon.
Dear Father, use me for Your glory as now,
forgiven, I can sing the songs of Zion.

Thank You, Lord, for allowing me to arise,
with mind intact, body healthy and whole.
For I know that waking up this morning,
was in the domain of Your full control.

September 8, 2000 - Friday

I WON'T BE THE SAME,

IN JESUS' NAME!

I won't be the same, in Jesus' name!
Victory is mine because of His great, selfless sacrifice.
I am pursuing peace with a vengeance, no more time for strife.

I won't be the same, in Jesus' name!
The enemy of my soul and his legions are all defeated foe.
I will fight victoriously, in the power of the Savior's might, I go.

I won't be the same, in Jesus' name!
I am whole, and filled with the fire of the Holy Ghost.
I will hold my head up high, purposefully striving, not on idle or coast.

I won't be the same, in Jesus' name!
Praying, in the Spirit, to snatch souls from hell's ghastly, flaming array.
Wanting all of my family and friends to join me in heaven, one day.

I won't be the same, in Jesus' name!
Stumping on the head of the enemy, crushing him under my feet.
Watching him scurry to and fro, looking for a temporary retreat.

I won't be the same, in Jesus' name!
Fear has no place in my life, or my heart, from this moment on.
I am fighting to have the mind of Christ, I want instability gone.

I won't be the same, in Jesus' name!
Looking back, second guessing my past, is a futile, time wasting game.
The Lord is coming back, I have no more time to be the companion of shame.

I won't be the same, in Jesus' name!
I will live and not die, neither will I be, ever again, mute or lame.
The seal of the Lord is upon my heart, His name I was created to proclaim.

October 2, 1999 - Saturday

I'VE GOTTA LIVE THIS THING

Psalm 51: 10 - 17
Create in me a clean heart, O God; and renew a right spirit within me.
Cast me not away from thy presence; and take not thy holy spirit from me.
Restore unto me the joy of thy salvation; and uphold me with thy free spirit.
Then will I teach transgressors thy ways; and sinners shall be converted unto thee.
Deliver me from bloodguiltiness, O God, thou God of my salvation: and my
tongue shall sing aloud of thy righteousness.   O Lord, open thou my lips;
and my mouth shall show forth thy praise.   For thou desirest not sacrifice;
else would I give it: thou delightest not in burnt offering.   The sacrifices of God
are a broken spirit: a broken and a contrite heart, O God, thou wilt not despise.

I've gotta live this thing.
Praising the Lord, makes my soul sing.
When I am down, His uplifting hands hold the peace I need.
I can't find that, in things, naturally acquired through greed.

I've gotta live this thing.
Worship boils down in my soul because Jesus' name does ring.
His love, like no other, fills the tiniest places in my tenderized heart.
Hey, there is nothing that you have to offer me, that will fulfill that part.

I've gotta live this thing.
Holding onto His garment's hem, I faithfully cling.
I am healed and set free, by His touch and His, alone.
I am alive today, because He answered my desperate moan.

I've gotta live this thing.
Whom else on this earth, can that type of lasting peace, bring?
My mind, rests safely, sane, secure, from the ravages of this age.
I am putting all of my faith in the Lord, as I travel along life's stage.

I've gotta live this thing.
I desire to stay under the loving, protective covering of Abba's wing.
Teach me, Holy Ghost, how to walk on this road of righteousness.
Show me what it is, I need to know and understand, in its fullness.

I've gotta live this thing.
He chose to love me, even when I was out having a fling.
Jesus knocked, I answered and glory to God, He came right in.
Ever since that time, He has just wanted to be my Lord and friend.

I've gotta live this thing.
I am single and whole, living for the Lord, my King.
Performing a transformation on a head, once as hard as wood.
I owe it all to Him, the Savior of my soul, the giver of everything good.

Yes, even in the face of trials and tribulations.
I, still, gotta live this thing.

September 6, 1999 – Tuesday

IN THE STILL OF THE NIGHT

Blanket of darkness, surrounds
your body in the still of the night.
I pray for you, as the Lord
Leads, for it is His delight.
I am asking the Father to,
right now, hold you tight.

I can sense that you stand in
need of His comforting touch.
He wants to shatter the delusion you
have, of depending on a fleshly crutch.
Instead, He wants you to know that no
one but He, could love you this much.

Now, you can safely turn over
and go right back to sleep.
He has promised this selfsame
hour, your weary soul to keep.
So rest in the assurance of His kind
of love, which runs eternally deep.

Lay your head on His bosom and
allow Him, you, to gently rock.
Let the stresses of the day dissolve,
relax, don't you dare look at that clock.
Close your eyes, now, trust in the Lord's
ability to not only tackle, but to block.

Climbing back into bed, curling up warm,
secure in the power of His might.
I have done what the Lord has asked
of me, so now I have put out the light.
My room is now in complete darkness,
for it is in the still of the night.

September 19, 2000 - Tuesday

J.O.Y.

Psalm 5: 11
But let all those that put their trust in thee rejoice:
let them ever shout for joy, because thou defendest them:
let them also that love thy name be joyful in thee.

Just praise, worship the King of kings
Justified, the blood of Jesus
Jealous God, exalt no other higher
Jump, twirl, dance before His throne
Jeans, slacks, sweats, suits, come as you are

Only believe, trust, hope
Oneness in the Spirit
Open heart, receive His love
Overcoming power, enemy defeated
One Lord, faith, baptism

Your sole hope, of salvation
You, hid securely, in Christ
Yelling, shouting victory's song
Yearly, daily, blessed beyond measure
Yielded vessel, contented, peaceful, loved

Zephaniah 3: 17
The LORD thy God in the midst of thee is mighty;
he will save, he will rejoice over thee with joy;
he will rest in his love, he will joy over thee with singing.

March 23, 1999 - Tuesday

LADY

You walk so tall, exuding elegance, style and grace.
Yet, not so tall, to stop and reach down, touching a child's face.

I am calling you higher and higher, My daughter, My love and My friend.
When they look at you, I don't want them to know where you start, and I end.

You are My lady and I have anointed you for this self-same hour.
The beauty, I have given you, is to be used to snatch souls
from the flames of hell, by My anointed power.

I know that I am your Lord, and you know that I go by many names.
Some of which are Jehovah, Abba, Savior, King, Comforter and Teacher;
no matter which one you use, I am, and will always be, the same.

Bless you, My child, the one called out before time could begin.
Now, that we have gotten to really know and love each other,
we will be together, one day, in the place where time has no end.

• • •

Hallelujah! Praise the Lord, sweet Jesus, for taking the time
to lovingly minister to my soul and make me, even more, this day, free.
Thank You, for blessing me so abundantly with Your holy, uncompromising
love, while letting me know that I am, first and foremost, Your lady.

February 7, 1999 – Sunday

LORD, THANK YOU FOR REMEMBERING ME

Luke 23: 32, 33, 39 - 43
And there were also two other, malefactors, led with him to be put to death.
And when they were come to the place, which is called Calvary, there they
crucified him, and the malefactors, one on the right hand, and the other on the left.
… And one of the malefactors which were hanged railed on him, saying,
If thou be Christ, save thyself and us. But the other answering rebuked him,
saying, Dost not thou fear God, seeing thou art in the same condemnation?
And we indeed justly; for we receive the due reward of our deeds: but this man
hath done nothing amiss. And he said unto Jesus, Lord, remember me
when thou comest into thy kingdom. And Jesus said unto him,
Verily I say unto thee, To day shalt thou be with me in paradise.

Dear LORD, You know that I am but a sinner saved by grace,
who though unworthy on my own merits, seeks a closer
walk with Thee, moment by moment, day by day.
I need You in every aspect of my life, not just for the
times of chaos, strife, family emergencies and the like,
but also in the times of joy, peace and rest, I pray.

Help me to continuously humble my heart, while seeking
Your divine forgiveness, as I repent for things done outside
of Your will, in supplication and holy reverence to Thee.
Teach me to walk worthy of this calling, You have so graciously
placed upon my life; continually, keep me under the shadow
of Your wings, which is the only place of true safety.

When my flesh rises up and wants things to be easy, bring back
to my remembrance the steps taken before You hung on that
cross to purchase salvation, healing and deliverance for me.
Continuously cleanse my heart, so the things I speak and write will
give an accurate testimonial of the overwhelmingly, compassionate love
of the only Savior, the Holy One, who gave His life to redeem all humanity.

Thank You, LORD!!!
Hallelujah and Amen!!!

October 2, 2017 – Monday

LOST AND FOUND

In a box?
Stole by fox?
Behind that lock?

In my haste
What a waste
One more taste

I lost my joy

Once so bright
Out went light
Doesn't seem right

I do care
Balloon without air
Where or where?

I lost my joy

Pain too strong
All night long
Vanquished my song

In darkness, blind
Troubled in mind
Peace cannot find

I lost my joy

Caught in sin
Let Jesus in
Repent, start again

Time to fast
Pray, at last
Fear, no past

I found my joy

Happy am I
One more try
The enemy, defy

Head, thorn crown
Blood seeped down
Staining the ground

I found my joy

Forgiven, once more
Hallelujah, praise outpour
Walking through door

Abba, mends heart
Bible teachings restart
Now set apart

I found my joy

Bible, daily peruse
Jesus, I choose
Winner, cannot lose

Holy Spirit led
Guilt, now dead
Unconditionally loved, instead

I found my joy

June 1, 1999 - Tuesday

MAKE ME WHOLE

Dear Lord, praise is
comely or so they say.
Help me, for sometimes I do
not feel like going that way.

My bed of affliction, caused
me to toss and turn.
Then right there, in the midst,
my heart started to burn.

The God of all comfort has
stepped in right on time, you see.
He came through, attended directly
to my problems, healed me.

The light of His love, soothingly
moved, taking control.
He began washing me
clean, He restored my soul.

Thank You, Lord, for the restful
peace that comes without toll.
Thank You, for showing how to
allow You to, again, make me whole.

May 26, 1999 - Wednesday

MUCH MORE THAN A NOTION

Lord, this praise is of the type that is
certainly much more than just a passing notion.
Move on us and through us, oh Lord, deep down
on the inside, like You do, Your mighty ocean.

Just as teeming life is abundant in the mighty seas,
and gravitates by Your majestic hand, towards to the shore.
Lord, fill my heart, and the heart of all those present, this night,
with Your abundant joy, so that we may praise You all the more.

In the future, when joy begins to wane, bring to our
remembrance all that You have delivered us from, in the past.
Lord, God, don't ever let us forget Your gracious mercy and Your love,
it's only in the remembrance of those things, that our praise for You, will last.

Lord, let praising and worshipping You, in my life,
and those whom I love, be much more than just a notion.
Fill our hearts and our lips with Your Spirit of gratitude as we
sincerely desire to give You, our full and complete devotion.

July 7, 1999 - Wednesday

MY HEART IS BLESSED BY YOU

My heart is blessed by You,
oh Lord, righteous, Holy One.
It is into Your divine, magnificent
presence, that I long to come.

Be blessed today,
my Lord, by this praise.
I am simply in awe of
Your mighty, loving ways.

The only power I command,
is from Your loving hands.
Teach me what it is I need to know,
to reach people from all lands.

In Your mercy and grace, may I
demonstrate to others the way to You.
Let compassion be my mainstay,
show me how to guide them through.

Blessed holy Father, the One from
whom I was given my very life.
I want to be ready when Christ returns,
His unstained bride, His wife.

Use me for Your glory;
may I never again, draw back.
Fill my cup, daily with the
nutrients of holiness that I lack.

You have blessed me over and over
again, by Your love, unconditional.
Dear Lord, I humble myself before You,
as I with You, become more personal.

Precious Holy Spirit continue to order
my steps as I, even now, stumble through.
It is due to Your unconditional love, that
my heart is wondrously blessed by You.

June 21, 2000 - Wednesday

MY HEART REACHES OUT TO THEE

My heart reaches
Out, oh Lord, to Thee
No other god, will
these eyes, I desire to see.

Lord, You have set
my soul on fire.
Loving You, exclusively,
has become my heart's desire.

Teach me Lord, to humbly
bow and to give You praise.
Show me how, oh Lord, to keep
focused on all of Your ways.

Line my spirit up, oh Lord,
with the words You preach.
Convict and correct me, Dear Lord,
between us, I want no breach.

Show me how to love You,
in the way that You deserve.
Keep me from wondering, as on this
highway of life, I sometimes swerve.

I want my heart to be single,
and my aim to be sure.
I want my heart to be cleansed,
that my thoughts may be pure.

As I stand, this morning,
before You, arms upraised.
I desire, oh Lord, to love You
for the remainder of my days.

The love that You have for me,
has taught me, oh so much.
I am better than the "old me", who
was so terribly bound up and such.

Thank You, Lord, for that is why
my heart reaches out to Thee.
I will praise no other, because You,
personally, came to set my soul free.

August 7, 1999 - Saturday

'NUF SAID

I
Love
Jesus
He
Loves
Me
'Nuf said

He
Hung
Bleed
Died
For
Me
'Nuf said

He
Rose
With
All-Power
In
Hand
'Nuf Said

He's
Available
To
All
Choose
Him
'Nuf said

He
Didn't
Have
To
Do
It
'Nuf said

July 28, 1999 – Wednesday

OH LORD, WE WORSHIP

AND ADORE, YOUR NAME

Oh Lord, we worship
and adore You.
We will place no other
gods before You.

For You, alone, bring
unspeakable joy to our hearts.
There is no way, from You,
we will ever depart.

You are more than the
wind beneath our wings.
You are our life's breath,
causing our hearts to sing.

We were created to worship
and praise You, Dear Lord.
Running this race, excites
our souls to the very core.

Standing here now, spirits aflame, as we
reverently offer up all that we have within.
Because, we know You, sweet Jesus,
paid the ultimate price for our sin.

Thank You, Lord, Jesus, for choosing us,
for we will never again be the same.
That is why, Oh Lord, we worship
and adore, Your name!

Hallelujah & Amen!!!

July 22, 1999 - Thursday

ON THE EDGE OF A PRAISE, FOR DAYS

I have been on the edge of a praise, for days.
Not the simple hallelujah, thank You, Lord type, oh no, no way.
The type where you are moved so deeply in your soul, words fail.

No words, eyes can only look inward as tears freely flow.
I am so completely, totally overwhelmed with His love, you know.
Holy Ghost, please continue to speak for me.

Let me just continue to rock right here, on the side of my bed.
With tears careening down my face, I can only shake my head.
Abba, I love You so very, very much.

My fingers are now moving on this computer's keys.
Desperately trying to capture this precious moment, in eternity.
Your Spirit calming my spirit, enveloping me in the purest love.

Lord, my life has not been easy, but I think about all that You have done.
My soul does more than cry out hallelujah, it melts with Your heart, into one.
Oh what a glorious, majestic wonder, full of compassionate love, You are.

Taking this once cast down soul, giving her the wings of the morning, to impart.
Dew kissed roses on a warm summer's day, nestle without thorns, within my heart.
The bitter shell of regret evaporates, now, like trapped steam, released in the air.

Showing me that no matter what the enemy brings to me, I do not have to fear it.
Thank You, heavenly Father, for this freedom and lightness in my spirit.
I have been floating on the waves of Your love, for years now.

Sometimes the ride has been choppy and even a little treacherous, at the end.
But, You have only been a faithful, loving guide, protector and friend.
I can only say that I love You, with all that is within me and I will never stop.

Dear Lord, please accept my humble attempt at worship and praise.
I have been on the edge of this real, down in the gut praise, for days.
Finally coming forth, being expressed from within my heart, upon this page.

October 20, 1998 - Tuesday

<u>OUTSIDE, INSIDE</u>

Matthew 28: 18 - 20
And Jesus came and spake unto them, saying,
All power is given unto me in heaven and in earth.
Go ye therefore, and teach all nations, baptizing them in the
name of the Father, and of the Son, and of the Holy Ghost:
Teaching them to observe all things whatsoever I have
commanded you: and, lo, I am with you alway,
even unto the end of the world. Amen.

Shut in, spiritually broke down,
in need of intensive care.
Lord, oh Lord, are You
really out there?

No, My darling, I am not out there,
but resting comfortably within.
My Dear Child, I love you and
I am still very much your friend.

Peace be still, I have come
to invite you to rest, now, in Me.
Let the shackles fall off, My Son,
Jesus, paid the price for your liberty.

Rise now, child, and acknowledge Him,
with passionate love, in all your ways.
Don't look for Me, outside of yourself,
look within, for I am with you, always.

May 26, 1999 - Wednesday

PRAISE IS COMELY

Psalm 147: 1
Praise ye the LORD: for it is good to sing praises
unto our God; for it is pleasant; and praise is comely.

The glow of love, moistens your face, your body temperature rises.
Praising your Lord, builds to a crescendo in your soul as high as the sky.
Unconscious of those around, who stare as if mystified.
No time to think, to get yourself "together", no time for fleshly pride.

Beautified in the Spirit of meekness, humbled in heart and mind.
Wanting all that the Lord has in store for you, not wanting to be left behind.
Allowing Him to love you, He tenderly caresses the deep hollows of your soul.
Wanting no more to be limited by circumstance, giving Him complete control.

Jump in, the water is just fine, it is heated by the Spirit of the Most High.
Don't just stand there staring at your inward circumstances, He knows you are not shy.
Jesus, has entered the room, stand up and give Him the praise, He is due.
You will find that your troubles will grow blessedly dim, learn to follow through.

This time of praise is also a time of teaching, delivering and setting free.
Wanting all that God has stored up, for such a time as this, to give to me.
Thank You, for the beauty of holiness and praise that exudes all around.
Learning to be silent, as well, in worship, seeking You while You may be found.

Glory to the Lord, hallelujah and hosanna, all rolled into one.
When I was in the world, I thought partying was fun.
Now, I have learned that joy bubbles in my soul, while my hands I raise.
I am allowing You to change my comeliness, You are teaching me to praise.

January 22, 1999 - Friday

PRAY, THEN GET OUT OF THE WAY

Pray, then get out of the way.
You don't even know the right words to say.
You say, "Yea", when you should have said, "Nay".

Pray, then get out of the way.
God is speaking, shut up and hear what He is trying to convey.
He is telling you to go right, but you choose left, this day.

Pray, then get out of the way.
The Lord has told you, that now is not the time to go, stay.
Plant yourself down, make no plans to move away.

Pray, then get out of the way.
Your baby is sick, do not dismay.
Lay them at the feet of the Master, let Him have His way.

Pray, then get out of the way.
You are worried because the bills are due, you have no money to pay.
The Lord already told you that He would see you through this disarray.

Pray, then get out of the way.
Jesus said that He would be with you, come what may.
Stop doubting Him, as you go recklessly astray.

Pray, then get out of the way.
Put your life completely under the care of the Holy Ghost, today.
Get comfortable, under the wings of Almighty God, do not delay.

You must learn to pray, then get out of the way.
Trust in the Lord with all of your heart, the sun is shining, go make some hay.
Allow the Father to clothe you in royal garments of priceless array.

Now, you have learned to pray and get out of the way.
The lessons of sweet rest and peace, have taken your burdens away.
Jesus, now Lord of your life, His blood, for your sins, a gift you can never repay.

April 30, 1999 - Friday

PRAYER CIRCLE

Prayer circle goes round and round.
Within the circle, loving comfort can be found.
Within the circle, comes deliverance, healing, joy and even pain.
Thank You, sweet Jesus, for the former and latter rain.

"Please, pray for me." they say, when all seems lost.
Praying to touch the heart of God, regardless of personal cost.
Soliciting prayer, for yourself, when strong knees become weak.
Knowing that with the best of intentions, you are not always humble and meek.

Needing the Lord to wrap His loving arms around you, your family and friends.
Strengthening you for the battle, just up ahead, right where the last victory did ascend.
Blessing the heart of God, by acknowledging the fact that without Him, you are nothing.
Allowing Him to wipe your tears, with a quickening that only His presence does bring.

You pray for me, Dear Friend, and I will pray for you, too.
The circle is never broken, because we desire to give the Lord, His due.
Surrender your heart to Him completely, as the Holy Ghost then directs your steps.
Then, come to His throne just as you are, without any unnecessary primping or prep.

Prayer circle goes round and round as we, in turn, enter into our Father's inner court.
The place where visions are manifested, directions are given, that flesh cannot abort.
Now that you have prayed and touched His heart, allow His love to wash you clean.
The prayer circle is never broken, for we need our Lord and Savior on whom we lean.

In Jesus' name, I pray. Amen and Amen!!!

May 9, 2000 - Tuesday

PREGNANT WITH A PROMISE

Something is growing
steadily inside of me.
Praying and fasting,
humbly bowing my knee.

Fear trying to take hold,
to draw me back to the past.
A time of empty promises
from man, that could not last.

But I can't give into it, I want to be
touched by Jesus, when He passes by.
I have decided to take God at His word,
because unlike man, He cannot lie.

Still memories are on parade inside my
head, fading but they certainly do die hard.
There is one, right over there beckoning to me,
like sun gleaming on a broken glass chard.

Remember the time when you held on,
and was left feeling dumb and abused?
Remember the time "so and so" said they
were your friend, then left you feeling used?

Taking out the garbage along with the
memories, trying to draw me back into the dark.
The Lord has come, again, answering my
distress signal, for I bear His heavenly mark.

Dispelling the darkness of lost hopes and
dreams, resealing them with a precious kiss.
Teaching me how to press on, to not miscarry;
I am after all, pregnant with His promise.

October 16, 2000 - Monday

RESCUE & RESTORATION

Cleansing fire, flood through my soul.
Father of the universe, to You, I relinquish control.
My will, this day, I humbly give to You.
Turn me away from the false dreams, I pursue.

Order my steps, as I seek Your face.
Be still my flesh, I need His grace.
Purify my heart, at its very core.
I truly desire to serve sin, no more.

Turning my plate down, seems no longer enough.
Reveal to me what still remains inside, including the ugly stuff.
Revelation comes in, tormenting my grasp on reality.
Jesus, sweet Jesus, surrounds my body with His, softly answering my pleas.

Thank You so much, Father, for the gift of Your Son.
Thank You for the hard fought battle, this victory just won.
Soul now set back on fire, mind has been freed.
Blessed Holy Ghost, thank You for revealing, to me, my need.

June 6, 1999 - Sunday

SET APART

Set apart for what?
All that keeps running through my mind is, but...
But Lord this, but Lord that
Now that I am here, where am I at?

Soft voice, speaking to my soul
Daring me to draw near, to cling, to hold
I am the Lord, your God, listen when I speak
The frustration has left my spirit, I am humble, now I am meek

The Lord, teaching me in the night seasons
Where darkness surrounds, with intent, with sinister reason
Wanting to pull me in permanently, to capture my soul, in hell
Speak up now, Lord, time is winding down, I can tell

I have set you apart to do My work
Stop flying off the handle, stop going berserk
Quiet your soul as you allow Me to love you, My child
I need you submitted, not running around buck wild

Go where I tell you, speak the words that I place in your mouth
Do not concern yourself with directions, you are headed south
Down, down, down to snatch souls from the flames
Let calmness envelop your soul, hear Me speak their names

Dear Heart, this is why I have called you
Your spirit and soul are now ready to follow through
I have healed your mind, your spirit, your body, your heart
Follow me, now, My child, you are washed in Jesus' blood, set apart

January 22, 1999 - Friday

SIMPLISTIC

Salvation and holiness, not at all complicated.
I sit here now, contented and satiated.
The Lord had come graciously to call.
He sustains with blessing, for one and all.

Took me in His arms, holding me close.
Telling me why He loves me, the most.
I cannot disagree, for my love is minuscule.
At times, being as stubborn as a mule.

Still, He loves me, even in the face of this negative trait.
He is the one, who has made my crooked places, straight.
Loving the Lord, becoming easier with each passing day.
Learning not to like what awaits me, when from Him, I stray.

Then, running back to my sweet Savior, I come, post haste.
Wanting to condemn myself, for the time that has been a waste.
Without rebuke, guilt or scorn, He welcomes me lovingly back.
We begin again, me forgiven, as though I never went off track.

Again, vowing not to let Him down, by following His commands.
Him reminding me, He made me from dust, I am but woman or man.
Humbling my soul to the point where I realize what is too lofty and unrealistic.
I could not take a breath without Him, much less live holy, it's just that simplistic.

October 13, 2000 - Friday

SING ME, A NEW SONG!

Sing Me, a new song
One that speaks about joy and liberty
Sing Me, a new song
Not about the things done, in bondage to the enemy

Sing Me, a new song
Let hallelujahs ring from bottom to top
Sing Me, a new song
Do not put Me on a time schedule, for a certain start or stop

Sing Me, a new song
Child, I have, for you, done a great many things
Sing Me, a new song
Lift your heart to Me, as your sacrifices you bring

Sing Me, a new song
Worship Me, no matter how tired your flesh may feel
Sing Me, a new song
How else will they know that My love, is for real?

Sing Me, a new song
Do not let disappointment still your lips, hindering My praise
Sing Me, a new song
Child, get in the birth position, snap out of tradition's haze

Sing Me, a new song
One that causes others to pause and take special note
Sing Me, a new song
Encourage others to launch out into the deep, in the Savior's boat

Child, just, "Sing Me, a new song!"

April 11, 2000 - Tuesday

SNAP!

Isaiah 61: 1 – 3
The spirit of the Lord GOD is upon me; because the LORD hath anointed me to preach
good tidings unto the meek; he hath sent me to bind up the brokenhearted, to proclaim
liberty to the captives, and the opening of the prison to them that are bound; To proclaim
the acceptable year of the LORD, and the day of vengeance of our God; to comfort all that
mourn; To appoint unto them that mourn in Zion, to give unto them beauty for ashes,
the oil of joy for mourning, the garment of praise for the spirit of heaviness; that they might
be called trees of righteousness, the planting of the LORD, that he might be glorified.

The speaker is winding down, coming to stand in front of the pulpit.
He is issuing an altar call, as lead by the Comforter, the Holy Spirit.
Now, I am stepping away from my seat, walking down the aisle.
It is time for serious business with the Lord, not a time to smile.

I stand there with arms raised in submission, laying myself bare.
Repentance is flowing from my lips, ignoring those, who simply stare.
How could I have given ear even a second, to manipulation's deceptive voice, again?
This time it came so subtlety, I could not recognize it, until it had me hemmed in.

Now, realization has come, with a healthy dose of understanding, minus the guilt.
The enemy had been actively trying to get me to doubt God, and go off full tilt.
Not so much as in a way that would actively draw concern, from true children of God.
Just enough to "hamstring" me, so that I would not go, when, God gave me the nod.

For in confusion, I would not be able to distinguish the voice of my sweet Lord.
While, running to and fro, sitting under some teachings, totally bored.
Thereby, rendering me ineffective to do what He had previously asked of me.
Not even realizing that all of this was bottling up, causing subconscious anxiety.

Now, at this altar, as the tears come and the tension in my heart begins to yield.
Hearing others crying all around me as in Your way, You prune and harvest their field.
Finally falling out under the power of the Holy Ghost, as a covering is placed over my lap.
I sense chains falling off me and, in the silence of my soul as they break, I hear them snap!

October 4, 2000 - Wednesday

SOMETHING HAS
COME OVER ME

Something has most
definitely come over me.
Causing once blinded
eyes, now, to see.

To see, what has always been there,
right in front of my face.
Seeing the One, who is the Giver
of all love, mercy and grace.

Grace that has kept me alive, when my
flesh simply wanted to die, or misbehave.
Fading into the night, lost
without hope of ever being saved.

Saved from the pain and hurt of a
childhood, that almost left me for dead.
Rescued by unseen hands, that tucked
ever so gently each night into bed.

A bed of torment, turned into one where
sweet dreams could come to play.
Annihilating the shackles of guilt and shame,
now before the Lord, truly dead, they lay.

Lay they must, now impotent to bring the
desired effect to a once oh, so willing mind.
Jesus has revealed Himself as the One,
who came to mend broken hearts, of all kind.

All kind and manner of brokenness, for He
came to this earth to set the captive free.
Taking a long time to realize that, one of
those captives was someone I used to be.

"Used to be", all glory goes to God, as no
sweeter words could flow through my brain.
I have been blessedly touched by the Lord,
with the former and the latter rain.

Latter rain flowing from the Lord as a refreshing,
cooling, transforming, healing spring of well water.
You have birthed, within the newness of my mended
heart, the unspeakable joy of being Your daughter.

Your daughter, once lost, now desires to
have continuous fellowship with Thee.
I will continue to praise You, for someone,
the Holy Ghost, has come over me.

October 16, 2000 - Monday

SOUL STIRRER

Came up to the pulpit
Head bowed in humility
A quiet, gentle dignity about himself
Opened God's Word, to begin to preach
More like teach, at first
The congregation listens
"Amen", flutters through the room
A few, "That's right. Yes, tell it.", do too
Very natural, relaxed in his presentation
Obviously, submitted to the Holy Spirit
Listening intently, not wanting to misstep
Painting pictures in our minds
Pictures of God's ability to be, right on time
Showing us, through the Word, how to stand still
That the battle truly does belong to the Lord

This message is really starting to take hold
People begin to stand to their feet
The teacher, now the preacher, raises his voice
Animated fully, by the power of the Lord flowing through him
The rest of the congregation senses God's Holy Presence
They stand, too, rising in agreement, claiming what God has for them
God has enlivened this man's spirit to preach a "right now" Word
To encourage the broken, the downtrodden
To lift the spirits of the saved, who are discouraged
To challenge those, who wish to remain in sin
To point the way of salvation, through the blood of Christ
To speak to the very nature of the Father, to heal
Willing to be a living witness, of the power of salvation
The power that miraculously transformed his once, destructive life
This preacher man, touched by the hand of the Master, is a soul stirrer

January 9, 2000 - Sunday

STAY OPEN AND STAY HONEST

Psalm 51: 15 - 17
O Lord, open thou my lips; and my mouth shall show forth thy praise. For thou desirest
not sacrifice; else would I give it: thou delightest not in burnt offering. The sacrifices of
God are a broken spirit: a broken and a contrite heart, O God, thou wilt not despise.

Romans 13: 12 - 14
The night is far spent, the day is at hand: let us therefore cast off the works of darkness, and
let us put on the armour of light. Let us walk honestly, as in the day; not in rioting and
drunkenness, not in chambering and wantonness, not in strife and envying. But put ye on
the Lord Jesus Christ, and make not provision for the flesh, to fulfil the lusts thereof.

Dear Lord, God, in Your Son, Jesus', name,
help me to stay open and honest before You.
When I hurt, help me to come straight to You,
for the help I must assuredly need to make it through.

Help me to boldly face my fears and not hide them away,
so that others will not see, be able to be a hindrance, or help to me.
Help me to humbly bring my soul into submission, with fasting and prayer,
so that I may stand proud and strong before You, not wavering like a new tree.

Never let me, again, seek the cover of darkness to bury
away things, and people, whom have caused me pain.
I give You permission, Holy Ghost, to draw me out in the open,
to be nurtured, cleansed and restored by Your healing rain.

Where else can I go, if not to You, Most Holy High Lord,
the Lover of my soul and Giver of my blessed life?
For there is no other, who will bear my burdens as You do,
going beyond the realm of father, mother, even husband and wife.

Dear Lord, help me to stay connected to the socket of Your everlasting love,
poured out for me, from Your never ending, miraculously healing fountain.
For I know that as I bring my hurts and pains to You, You, alone, are the One,
who will bring me out of that valley, placing me back on the top of this mountain.

Amen

October 21, 2000 - Saturday

79

SWITCH IN THE SPIRIT

Called on another fast
Water only, this time
Food all around
Wherever I looked
Got to work, someone
A cake placed on the table
Broke that fast
Got home and cooked

Called to another fast
Water only this time
Didn't want any food
Didn't even want to go near it
This time, successfully
Made it through
I know why that happened
God flipped the switch in my spirit

October 18, 1998 - Sunday

THANK YOU, FOR THE
VISITATION, LORD

Thank You, for the visitation, Lord, You
knew I really longed for that special touch.
Thank You, for prompting the heart of my friend,
who took the time to call me at that precise moment.
Blessed Lord, that is why praising and worshipping
You, for either of us, is never enough or too much.

Thank You for that visitation, Lord,
it is one I never want to forget.
In that call, she shared Your Word, from
2 Peter 3, verses one through eight.
Your timing is absolutely perfect, for in times like
these, Your Spirit and ours, have more intimately met.

Thank You, for the visitation, Lord, for that
confirming Word, fertilized previous seed.
You touched our souls in such a way, that as joy
bubbled up inside, as we began to worship and praise.
Lord, You are so lovingly kind, here I was, alone, praying for
others, and You chose my sister to speak directly to my need.

Thank You, Lord!

2 Peter 3:1 – 8

This second epistle, beloved, I now write unto you; in both which I stir up your pure minds by way of remembrance: That ye may be mindful of the words which were spoken before by the holy prophets, and of the commandment of us the apostles of the Lord and Saviour: Knowing this first, that there shall come in the last days scoffers, walking after their own lusts, And saying, Where is the promise of his coming? for since the fathers fell asleep, all things continue as they were from the beginning of the creation. For this they willingly are ignorant of, that by the word of God the heavens were of old, and the earth standing out of the water and in the water: Whereby the world that then was, being overflowed with water, perished: But the heavens and the earth, which are now, by the same word are kept in store, reserved unto fire against the day of judgment and perdition of ungodly men. But, beloved, be not ignorant of this one thing, that one day is with the Lord as a thousand years, and a thousand years as one day.

April 19, 2000 - Wednesday

"THAT MUCH"

Right in the middle
of getting ready to go.
God touches my heart
and gently says, "No".

There is something that
He wants to convey.
He is taking me to my
knees, to listen, to pray.

I say, "Speak to me, Lord,
bring peace to my mind.
Reveal to me what You will,
whatever You find."

He replies, "I long for you,
My child, I just needed your touch.
I did not want you to leave this house,
today, without knowing,

I love you, that much."

June 6, 1999 - Sunday

THE GAP STANDER!

Ezekiel 22: 30
And I sought for a man among them,
that should make up the hedge, and
stand in the gap before me for the land,
that I should not destroy it: but I found none.

These words have brought tears to my eyes.
I just received news that has caused me to sigh.
Lord, have mercy, someone in need of salvation, is sick and near death.
I will pray for Your healing touch, as long as You give me the breath.

Ours is not to question Your will, but to call for it to be done.
Not all of Your gifts bring us joy, for You, alone, are the Holy One.
If I was in charge of this world, what a mess it would be in.
I would spare the lives of all of my family and those I call, friend.

But, our ways are not yours, for our hearts are too easily swayed.
We, change our minds so fast, that we forget for what we have just prayed.
When we receive it, we cringe and wonder what could have possible been on Your mind.
Yet, You simply were answering the requests that we made of the desperate kind.

Thank You, sweet merciful Lord, for leaving the care of the world, right where it belongs.
Teach me the prayers of the righteous, as led by the Holy Ghost, through my night songs.
Lord, now this need has come squarely to my door and resides firmly in my lap.
Lord, help me to kneel in honest prayer and submission to You, while I stand in the gap.

September 17, 1999 – Friday

THIS JESUS...

This Jesus
Who walked on water, calming the raging sea
Who, in omnipotent authority, set the captives free
Who told the devil, the enemy, he had to flee
Who paid the price, in His own blood, for our liberty

This Jesus
Who, in love and compassion, made the blind to see
Who healed the mentally and physically infirmed, changing their destiny
Who was born of a virgin and the Holy Spirit, to save you and me
Who, in the midst of a life-threatening storm, slept like a baby

This Jesus
Only Begotten Son of the Father, Creator of all that was, is now, and will ever be
Son of righteousness, obedient unto death, accepting His fate with humility
Bright and Morning Star, more than worthy of all power, honor and glory
LORD and Savior, leading all who belong to Him, in predestined victory

This Jesus!

September 8, 2017 – Friday

TOO BLESSED TO BE DEPRESSED!

PSALM 5: 11 & 12
But let all those that put their trust in thee rejoice: let them ever shout for joy, because
thou defendest them: let them also that love thy name be joyful in thee. For thou,
LORD, wilt bless the righteous; with favour wilt thou compass him as with a shield.

Hallelujah! Blessed be the name of the Lord!
My heart is pumping in pure joy, on one heavenly accord.
The Lord is my King, my Savior and my beloved Friend.
This joy has captured my spirit, sanctifying it from deeply within.

Hallelujah! Blessed beyond measure, beyond all hope.
Feet given the wings of the morning, no stress of which, together, we cannot cope.
Abba has bathed me in His love and adored me, since before time could begin.
Whirling around this room, shouting out my love for Him, signifying the state that I am in.

Hallelujah! Blessed to the very depths of a once battered, lonely soul.
Body, now, realigned to offer up praises to my Lord, far beyond human control.
To the world, my heart should be heavy, Christmas is coming, without children or mate.
Glory be to God for His love is massaging the cockles of my being, this very date.

Hallelujah! Blessed to the point of feeling His arms surrounding me like a sleeping bag.
Tingling at His touch, as I skip along in the spirit, like a child joyfully playing tag.
It is not that I do not desire to have children or a mate one of these days, for I do.
Casting out doubt, instead choosing to praise God for all that He has brought me through.

Hallelujah! Blessed and relaxing, all curled up in the hem of Jehovah-Jireh's garment.
Not letting the enemy win this battle for possession of my soul, leading me to torment.
It is more than a cute saying on a bumper sticker, designed by someone to alleviate stress.
I am loved beyond measure by the Holy Trinity, I am too blessed to be depressed!

December 23, 1999 – Thursday

TROUBLE HEALED

Troubled heart
Troubled mind
Troubled soul
Give Jesus full control

No need to fight
Victory brings light
Stand up for what is right
The Holy Spirit will see you through the night

Lord, I pray, give them strength
Let them seek You, no matter the length
It is most certainly time well spent
Jesus came, the veil of darkness did rent

Just raise your hands in total surrender
Father's mercies toward you are new and tender
Do not fear the One, who is the heart mender
The great I AM is calling you, don't be a pretender

Healed heart
Healed mind
Healed soul
Jesus, now, has full control

Blessed Be The Name Of The Lord!!!

May 31, 2000 - Wednesday

UNITE MY HEART

Psalm 86: 11-12
Teach me thy way, O Lord; I will walk in thy truth:
unite my heart to fear thy name! I will praise thee, O Lord my God,
with all my heart: and I will glorify thy name for evermore.

Unite my heart with Yours, oh Lord,
teach me how to wait on You.
Show me how not to rush in on wings of flesh,
crashing head long, disastrously through.

Teach me how to live at the level of anointing,
that You have sovereignly placed upon me.
Then, guide my steps as I learn to confidently,
in You, seek to set the captives free.

Let my voice be the voice of love,
praise, worship and hope, not of doom.
Help me to call forth the things from death to life,
like You did, sweet Jesus, for Lazarus in the tomb.

With all that is within me, I desire to obtain
a new, closer walk in Spirit and in truth.
I do not want to have to hide the choices that I make,
like someone behind the curtain of a voting booth.

Lord, use me for Your divine glory,
teach me to get out of my own, way.
Remind me, in times of uncertainty, especially,
not to give an answer, before I pray.

May 16, 2000 - Tuesday

WATERING

Jeremiah 17: 7 – 8
Blessed is the man that trusteth in the LORD, and whose hopethe LORD is.
For he shall be as a tree planted by the waters, and that spreadeth out her roots
by the river, and shall not see when heat cometh, but her leaf shall be green;
and shall not be careful in the year of drought, neither shall cease from yielding fruit.

God, our Father's, nature is watering the death out of my life.
The gentleness of His love for me is as calming as a summer's wind.
The colors in God's creation are enlivening my spirit as joy floods my being.
Take a moment to look around you, for all things speak to His presence within.

Tempting fate, as the world would say.
Speaking of just how good the Lord has truly been.
Lay that aside and jump in, Dear Heart, the water is fine.
For you see, "No one can do you like Jesus", my friend.

Praise frolicking, cart wheeling ever so gently through my heart.
Sometimes, I feel like I could just spend all day caught up in His love.
But, the cares of the world come to keep me firmly planted in today.
Still, I long for the washing of His love upon my soul, tenderly given from above.

Okay, it took you long enough, but you finally figured it out, I do really love the Lord.
He is more to me than just a quick, "Thank You" and "Help me", when I am in need.
He fills the very confines of my spirit, as it stretches right back to encapsulate Him.
For, you see, when He hung on that tree for my sins, His flesh surely did bleed.

There is so much about Him that I could not possibly know, no matter how long I live.
I am determined not only to love Him with my mind, but also with body, soul and heart.
He will be whatever you need Him to be, but He will only come as close as you allow.
Know in your spirit, that you want His love pumping through your soul as a vital part.

Allow the Holy Ghost to comfort you, as He teaches you about Their love for us.
Don't be afraid, unwrap the package that is sealed with the imprint of a dove.
Blessings, my triune Lord, for all that You have so patiently done in my very core.
Thank You, Jehovah, for watering, washing my soul clean, teaching me how to love.

July 28, 1999 – Wednesday

88

WE WIN!

Split second, prayer
"Help"

God answers

Fear, exposed runs

Peace comes

Joy restored

Clarity revealed

Love floods heart

Jesus stepped in

On His face, a big grin

Reminding us

Yet, again
We win!

June 6, 1999 - Sunday

WHAT'S NEXT!?

Dear Lord, Your promises are bearing
much fruit and are being harvested, at last.
I, now, know for a certainty that I am the
head and not the tail, like I was in my past.

Songs of praise, worship and poetic
utterances course through my heart.
I am no longer a victim of circumstance,
constantly being hit with the enemy's darts.

Sure they still come, but You have
lifted up a standard against them.
The enemy has had to flee seven
different ways, because of his fear of Him.

Him, being the Savior, the one, who
came to this earth just to set our souls free.
The Holy One, who created this new heart
of devotion, determination and destiny.

I hear You calling me to a level, higher
than any to which I could previously reach.
There are those, who doubt this call, but
I am to absorb, only, what You have to teach.

No other voice will I follow, my Comforter,
for I am no longer a goat, but a sheep.
I have gotten off of the world's roller coaster,
which caused my very spirit to weep.

Through my pain and heartache, You've
used me to deliver, restore and make whole.
I give You all of the glory, taking none
for myself, while operating in this ministry role.

Continue to ignite my soul with praise
and adoration, teach me to keep a firm hold.
Just like a horse with a bit in its mouth, lead
me where You, predestined I should go.

Soften my tongue as Your righteous Son's
blood, through my veins continues to flow.
Teach me the lessons in Your instructor's
manual, put together to help me to grow.

I have been walking in Your divine
anointing, for quite a few years, now.
One of the hardest lessons that I ever
learned, was how to, to You, humbly bow.

I bowed down my pride, my expectations,
the foolhardy desires of a lost child.
Because, You have shown me how,
in surrender, I could be meek and mild.

My desire now is to go as
far, in You, as You will allow.
I want to obtain unbroken fellowship
with You, Lord, just show me how.

Draw me near, oh Lord, as near
as the next breath that I will inhale.
I have to stay on this course, I willingly
choose no other alternative route to sail.

However, this new phase of my anointing
has found me, without a script or a text.
I am yielding my will to Yours, Father, as You
expand my vision to see, what's next!

July 19, 1999 - Monday

WHILE I HAVE MY BEING

Psalm 104: 33
I will sing unto the LORD as long as I live:
I will sing praise to my God while I have my being.

While I have my being, this one,
gifted to me by the Lord;
I will sing of His goodness, which
has blessed me beyond reward.

I will sing until my lungs can
no longer support a note.
I will sing regardless of whether
you deem me fit, by human vote.

I will sing the heavens down, allowing
the glory of the Lord to become my cloak.
I will sing of His power and how He has come
down to, the enemy's privileges, revoke.

I will sing to you, whether you want to
hear me or not, because it is for Him, I sing.
I will sing because He has not only given
me this life, but He is my sovereign King.

I will sing until there are no more
words left to flow through this brain.
I will sing until, in your life, you surrender
to the Lord and allow Him free reign.

I will sing in a way that brings praise
to His heart and blesses His very soul.
I will sing in the free style of a heart touched
by God, and under His majestic control.

I will sing until you join me, with
a heavenly chorus all of your own.
I will sing, with you then, because
I will know in your heart, He is enthroned.

I will sing until every member of my family
has humbled their hearts to my Savior.
I will sing of His righteous goodness,
which can curb any foolhardy behavior.

I will sing often and I will sing loud, until the
Lord comes to take my soul to heaven.
I will then lay aside this mantle, so that you
can sing against partaking of strange leaven.

I will sing until the very breath
in this body has taken its leave.
I will sing in the spirit as I rise up
heavenward, to His hem I will cleave.

Yet, that time is not now, so while
I have my being, I will sing of His praise.
I will sing for all He has done for me, and
out of gratitude and love, this voice I raise.

October 28, 2000 - Saturday

WIPE THE TEARS FROM YOUR EYES

Jeremiah 31: 3
"The LORD hath appeared of old unto me, saying, Yea, I have loved thee
with an everlasting love: therefore with lovingkindness have I drawn thee."

Dear One, you must know that I love you with an everlasting love,
so come to Jesus and let Him wipe the tears from your eyes.
Shame has no place, for He has not come to condemn you,
but to tenderly bring you closer to His bleeding side.

All the times when you ran from Him in search of
other arms and things to fill the emptiness in your heart;
He stood lovingly by and waited patiently for you
to repent, and from that form of love, depart.

Surely, you have come to realize, now, that once obtained,
love cannot be sustained, unless He is in the midst of it.
In the midst of all situations, no matter what they may be, for
only when obtained in His love, will there be unity of the Spirit.

His desire for you is that you live in peace and harmony,
while learning to valiantly fight the good fight of faith in His might.
He will be there for you always, through the good and the bad,
no matter how pressing the darkness, He is there with you in the night.

•   •   •

I am the giver of light and life, and all things created
under heaven and earth, have been created by divine touch.
I hold you in the hollow of My hand to protect you from storms,
when they rage against you, breaking up confusion, despair and such.

I know that your heart is hurting and that no amount of man contrived
dialect or dissertation, will still the emptiness, that now threatens to consume.
Know that you are Mine, My child, and the enemy as a defeated foe,
is trying to get your attention, by hollering at you from an empty tomb.

For My Son is no longer there, as you well know, and deception and tricks
are all that this enemy has left in the arsenal, lying impotent on the roadside.
Now, rebuke those feelings and thoughts in the name of My Son, Jesus, and walk
out into the light of His Son-shine, allowing Him to wipe the tears from your eyes.

July 28, 2000 - Friday

YOUR SHINING LOVE

Your shining love
Pulsates through my soul.
In its wake, false
has lost its hold.

Foolishness, no longer
tolerated, has flown the coop.
Now I can walk tall, filled with
Your fire, no longer in a stoop.

Your divine love has captured me
completely, and I won't let You go.
No one, can come between us, now,
Lord, for each day, closer, we grow.

Oh, what joy is tumbling,
childlike, freely through my heart.
Good God, Almighty, thank You,
or making my life Your creation of art.

I flow in ways that only Your omniscient,
loving hand could have designed.
I have searched all over, but no other
love has ever sustained, like your kind.

Continue to cleanse my heart, mind,
body and soul, each and every part.
Leave no stone unturned, root out anything
that would come up, to keep us apart.

My spirit loves to sing Your praises, my
mouth lifts sweet songs of worship, too.
Lord, have mercy, I can barely contain
myself, what am I supposed to do?

Let me take a minute, right now,
and get up out of this chair.
I am in my own office, there is
no one to interrupt me, or to stare.

Excuse me, for a few moments, as I allow
that beat to flow and alter my stance.
That felt totally great, Lord, thank You, for my
heart now beats to the rhythm of that dance.

My fingers are being led, by the love that
I feel for You, to flow across these keys.
My only desire, is to be found in Your sight,
as one, in whom, You are well pleased.

Blessed be Your holy name, my Father,
Savior, Comforter, sweet heavenly dove.
Words fail to adequately describe, how it really
feels to be enveloped in Your shining love.

February 5, 1999 – Friday

YOUR WILL

Today, before I could put the finishing touches on the 2nd Edition of
"While I Have My Being", I heard You, Dear LORD, speaking of
the need for razor sharp focus and humility, ever so gently to my soul.
I could see the book as pages flipped through the screen of my mind,
and this was the last poem to be included, all these years later,
in this continuously fluid journey, towards my predestined goal.

Earlier in the morning, as I was reading Psalm 25,
the idea of Your paths being formed of mercy and truth,
sunk in really deep in my spirit and took an earnest foothold.
There are times, when the knowledge of the great sacrifice that
Your Son, Jesus, made by willingly going to that cross, breaks my
heart to the extent that I desire for it to fervently run hot, never cold.

As I began to rise, I found a note that I had written in April of 1997 and
it alluded to my need, at that time, to prepare for a very specific season
in my life, that made me a bit nervous, at the time, but never took place.
I sat there somewhat stunned as I continued to read it, realizing that I had
allowed my fear, at that time, to cause me to be distracted by false lights
and go trotting off, off-course, stumbling and falling in that particular race.

Thank You, LORD, for Your unconditional love, grace and mercy, for You have
truly brought me a mighty long way, while pouring in the comfort that only come
from Holy Spirit; especially, when I foolishly relied on my own finite intellect and skill.
Thank You, Heavenly Father, for once again, patiently teaching me to humble my heart
before You, repenting and seeking forgiveness, in holy consecration and submission,
as I stay the course, to press in, and hear Your still small voice, speak again, of Your will.

October 2, 2017 – Monday

<u>YOUR TOUCH</u>

There is nothing like Your touch, upon my skin
The warming glow that it imprints, upon my heart
Nothing can compete with it, nothing ever will

Love wrapped up in a Comforter, so divine
Love nailed to a cross, to save my soul from hell
Love directed from on high, our Father's home

Mighty in valor, as pure as jewels untouched by man
Omnipotent, omniscient, omnipresent
Wanting only my love, in return

Enabling me to love in ways, not known by unsaved man
Freeing my soul to soar, yet grounded to serve
Touching not only with my hand, but His Spirit within

Lord, forgive my sins and cleanse my heart
Jehovah, take not Your Holy Spirit from me
Abba, I would die, without Your touch

January 22, 1999 - Friday

IN CONCLUSION

In conclusion of this matter, I would like to say that I hope, and pray, these small offerings were found acceptable in the sight of God, first and foremost, then man. I do not claim to be a poet, with all knowledge of meter and rhyme, just a psalmist, who loves the LORD, and desires with all that is within, to capture in writing, what it is He is speaking to my heart and vice versa. I trust, I have conveyed that in a coherent, Godly manner. In the sincerest sense, my desire is, that your heart, through the reading of these poems, was made, will be made, more tender towards the LORD. If you are not a Christian, I pray that in the reading, you found at least a grain of truth that you could not challenge, or escape that grabbed ahold of your heart. I also pray that the love the LORD has for you, was more than made evident, in at least a line or two. For as the old saying goes, "If He did it for me. I know He will do it for you". You just have to trust Him. His love will do the rest!

I have been a Christian since 1984, when I first called out to Jesus to save me, in the midst of a separation that led to a subsequent divorce. I confess, I have most assuredly stumbled more than my fair share of times, over the years. Yet, in all that stumbling, I have never once been cast aside by the LORD. I have, however, turned my back on Him; even though, He has never turned His back on me. His love is unconditional, and I will forever praise Him for that fact! I also know, for a fact, that His grace is truly sufficient and I count on it being so, moment by moment, as I go about each day.

I further pray that, if you had an area of need, it was touched upon by something written here or within the previous pages. This project was, for me, one bathed in love, grace, worship, revelation, healing and deliverance. After editing and re-editing these poems, and everything else that this book contains, one word kept flooding through my soul, while tears moistened my eyes. That word was, and remains, "Hallelujah!" God is just simply that good, and I thank Him for bringing While I Have My Being *(1ˢᵗ Edition and, now, the 2ⁿᵈ Edition)* to fruition. It is a promised fulfilled, again!

One other thing, I feel I must add before I close.   In the creative process, at times, I have found that I can stop whatever I am doing, and catch thoughts in writing, right as they flow through my mind. Still, at other times, I am driving here or there, listening to a sermon, or doing something else, that cannot be put on hold, and I have to pray and ask the LORD to bring those words, and verses, back to my mind, at a more opportune time. I have come to the contented realization, if He intended that those words, or songs, reach paper and pen, or computer screen, they will. Some things, I have had to learn, and accept, will remain just between us, and will never be seen in print. They are simply, if you will, praise and worship songs sung in the spirit of love and adoration, I have for the LORD. I liken it to catching a glimpse of a really beautiful butterfly, then deciding to run and get your camera to take a picture of it, only to find that it has flown away. In its wake, it has left only the wondrous memory of its presence in your life, for that brief moment.

May you also sing love songs to the LORD, in your own special way. May you never give up on the dreams that the LORD is, or has, birthed in your heart that will press through your soul in whatever way He so chooses. To God be the glory, forever and always!!! In Jesus' name and by His shed blood, I pray! Hallelujah and Amen!!!

In His Gracious, Merciful Love & Service,
Michelle Louise Pierre
March 28, 2002 – Wednesday
Revised for 2ⁿᵈ Edition – October 2, 2017 – Monday

ABOUT THE AUTHOR

Michelle, a born-again Christian and a native San Franciscan *(who also spent two years of her school-aged years in New Orleans, LA, while living with her maternal grandmother)*, has authored several more books of poetry, as mentioned in the "Introduction", in addition to this one. However, this is the first one that was selected for publication. She is an avid reader and prolific writer, who took to heart, advice she was given, after having a non-fiction short story accepted by a magazine, then completely re-edited before publication, without her permission. The advice was simple, "Learn from the experience, copyright everything, and no matter what, keep writing."

Michelle currently resides in Hayward, California, with her nearly 10 year old kitties, Buttons and Coco, littermates. She adopted them when they were nine and a half weeks old. They are a constant source of love, companionship and entertainment, all rolled into two; especially, when they are not cat-napping. After graduating from Lowell High School in San Francisco, she went on to attend San Jose State University where she obtained a B.A., C.R.S. Credential, and M.A. in Speech Pathology and Audiology. She is a licensed Speech Therapist, who remains single, after a divorce many moons ago, with all the benefits that entails. Michelle is also now retired from the Hayward Unified School District *(combined public service with East Side Union High School District, Cupertino Unified and Alum Rock Unified of over thirty years – during which, she worked with students from the ages of three to twenty-one)*. She also worked for nearly two years, on a contract basis, with the zero to three population. Michelle enjoyed that season of her life and now is thoroughly embracing this new season *(Employed people often ask her how she feels about being retired. Her answer is a resounding, "I love it! It is great to do what you want to do, when you want to do it; and, if that means doing nothing at all, that is okay, too." That statement is usually followed by a very hearty laugh)*.

Some of Michelle's other interests include: singing, playing her tambourine, dancing, sewing, crocheting, photography *(cover photos were taken by the author)*, wood working, playing around with technology and gardening, as well as ministering the Word of God to groups of fellow Christian singles, women and within other small group settings. Michelle has also recently overcome one of her "fears" and discovered a passion for line dancing.

Notes and/or Insights